During his nearly thirty years of service in the House, Congressman Jim McDermott offered a bold progressive voice for working families. Whether championing single payer health care, fighting for a public option or combating HIV/AIDS, he fought to secure quality, affordable health care for all. In his compelling memoir, Congressman McDermott grapples honestly with the realities of holding public office and what it means to serve the American people. All those passionate about public service will benefit from his sharp insight and thoughtful candor.
— *Nancy Pelosi, Speaker of the House*
(Congressman, 1987–Present)

Jim McDermott writes with the insight of a psychiatrist, the experience of a legislative pro, and the wit and charm of an Irish raconteur. In his frank style he shows us how Congress became broken and corrupted. He calls for a more democratic and humane Congress that works for a more just society and where we can begin once again to listen to each other and, *con-egresso*, come together. I thoroughly enjoyed reading and learning from one of the best to have graced the US Capitol.
— *David Bonior, Congressman and Congressional leader*
(1977–2003)

In politics, as in life, the battles we thought we had won don't stay won. From voting rights, to abortion rights, to LGBTQ+ rights, to union rights, eternal vigilance is required, especially from those who serve. Jim McDermott "got it" and persevered for 28 years in Congress. In *Money, Love, & Power*, McDermott provides candid insights into what makes politicians tick, providing an insider's perspective on our divisive politics. A worthwhile, unique book.
— *Mazie Hirono, US Senator (2013–Present)*

I feel as if I have had a college course in American politics and found it fascinating. I'm sure any student or young politician with ambitions to enter Congress will find it invaluable. It's also of interest to those of us abroad who want to understand how the place works. It is very different from our own idiosyncratic Parliament.
— *Baroness Joan Walmsley, House of Lords, UK*

With a psychiatrist's sagacity and wisdom acquired over half a century serving in the Washington State and US legislatures, Jim McDermott describes in clear, simple, and honest language what motivates and frustrates the professional politician. If you want to understand what lies behind the media grandstanding, what it's really like to raise money for campaigns and then deal with the "asks" that entails, and why good people still serve despite the profession's pitfalls and the toll on their lives, read this book.
— *Karl Marlantes, Author and Vietnam War veteran*

Jim McDermott was a wonderful House colleague — affable and empathetic, a great raconteur, deeply serious in purpose, quick to spot the cant and rationalizations common in politics. All of these qualities are on display in *Money, Love, & Power*. The book is replete with wry observations, sharp insights, and astute advice, informed throughout by concern for the condition and prospects of our democratic institutions.
— *David Price, Congressman (1987–Present)*

The essence of McDermott's 28 years in Congress is distilled into this delight of a book. It explores the wisdom gained from this experience, the practical exigencies of Congressional life, and the impact of its very real demands on those who decide to enter politics. Its value transcends national borders. For those thinking of entering a political arena, it will help in their preparation for the unexpected and the unfair, especially for the inevitable attacks on one's integrity and moral sense. Anyone interested in political life will appreciate its gems.
— *Elizabeth Reid, First Adviser to a Head of Government, Australia, on matters relating to women and children (1973–1975)*

A candid account of the voyage by a seasoned Congressman through the labyrinth of American politics. The insightful narration should serve both freshmen and the experienced to navigate the landscape.
— *Prasad Kunduri, Former Fulbright-APSA Congressional Fellow*

I broke out in a cold sweat when reading, in one sitting, *Money, Love, & Power*. It brought back the gut-wrenching realities of pressures and temptations and even some failures around the "money issue." More than in fundraising itself was the shadowy and camouflaged temptations of being subject to attractive influence peddling. Rarely did any of us in the "sausage making factory" reveal the trauma of what it means to be in the noise and dirt ("strum and dang") of the industry's machinery, as Jim has in this expose. If you read this book you may not run for Congress. If you don't read it you may run for Congress, win a seat, and regret one day not knowing what is in these pages, and in the hearts of many who preceded you.
— *Thomas R. Getman, Legislative Director to Senator Mark O. Hatfield (1979–1985)*

With revealing honestly borne insights, the author acknowledged that for "politicians everything is about us" and "how we appear to the public." Referencing the early wisdom of nineteenth century physician, William Osler, Jim spoke of the need to listen to patient's stories, and by inference his constituents. The book touches on the evolving impossibility of bipartisan legislation, and the rise of autocracy where truth is a disposal product. I would definitely recommend this book as an essential primer for political science students, would be politicians, and even lawyers.
— *Kieran D. O'Malley, MD, Distinguished Life Member American Academy of Child and Adolescent Psychiatry, Retired Fellow Royal Society Medicine, and Poet*

Money, Love, & Power

A Guide to
Understanding Congress

Money, Love, & Power

A GUIDE TO
UNDERSTANDING CONGRESS

by

JIM MCDERMOTT

Money, Love, and Power
A Guide to Understanding Congress

   seamus7474@gmail.com

Money, Love, and Power: A Guide to Understanding Congress

ISBN: 978-0-578-29272-4

BOOK & COVER DESIGNS: WARD STREET PRESS
BOOK PRODUCTION: WARD STREET PRESS
FRONT COVER PHOTO: JAY MURPHY
BACK COVER AUTHOR PORTRAIT: JEAN-AUGUSTE LOBARTHE-PIOL

THIS BOOK IS DEDICATED TO
Wayne Morse
Ernest Gruening
& Karl Marlantes

TABLE OF CONTENTS
✻

Money, Love, & Power

A Guide to
Understanding Congress

FOREWORD

IN BEGINNING TO WRITE a book, one should consider who might read the book. I expect this book will be read by students, adults, political scientists, newspaper reporters and television reporters, and politicians. To understand politicians, you have to realize that everything is about us. The only thing that matters is how we appear in the public mind.

Much of what we do and all of what we say is designed, one way or another, to lead to election and reelection. Image creation is a continuous process in which all politicians are engaged all the time. Let me stop here to let you in on the secret. Every politician who has seen this book has immediately turned to the index to see if his or her name is contained there.

This is not a phenomenon solely represented by politicians. All famous people turn immediately to the index to see if they're included, if they believe the book intersects with their lives.

Most politicians will not have read this forward before they turn to the back of the book to see if part of their life story is reported herein. To those politicians who were not included by name in this book, I apologize. I've used your stories and adapted them in thousands of ways in this book. Without my colleagues, this book would not be possible nor would it be necessary.

Trying to understand how politicians think, and subsequently how they behave is a complicated process. Often, unfortunately, they behave and then they think. The old maxim that you can't get in trouble for things you didn't say is often ignored by a politician who wants to be quoted or be noticed. As politicians get older, and hopefully wiser, they ponder more before they speak.

A good editor is someone who could take out the things that shouldn't be said. In that spirit, I have waited to write this book until the end of my career because I wanted to be free to say things that might have created problems for me in the past. Since my career is at an end, I can now say what I have observed with no fear. I will not have to pay on the floor of the House or in the committee room for my observations and interpretations of my colleagues' behaviors. In summary, this book is intended to educate people so they understand their representative's motivations, and with that knowledge they can participate in the political process knowing some of their secrets.

Jim McDermott
Seattle, Washington

INTRODUCTION:
NO ONE GOES TO
CONGRESS TO BECOME
A SCOUNDREL

As I WATCHED THE Michael Cohen hearings before the Oversight Committee of the House of Representatives, I couldn't help thinking of an essay from a don at Oxford, C.S. Lewis, entitled, *The Inner Ring*. It should be required reading for every member of Congress before they start a new session.

Lewis lays out for the King's College, University of London graduates, the path a person follows to become a scoundrel. Commencement addresses usually look to present a bright future in front of the graduates. Lewis chooses to follow a different line of thought.

Instead, he talks about a path some will take, even though they are not planning to do so. People rarely directly seek to become a scoundrel but rather, they evolve gradually into the state in which Michael Cohen finds himself today. The process is gradual and incremental and almost imperceptible as a person slips from being an honorable person into becoming totally dishonorable and discredited.

The desire to be in the inner ring, in some aspect of one's society, is almost universal. To be accepted and trusted and admired by one's peers is a state that all members of Congress want to attain. It is a state one must reach if you are to be re-elected and accumulate power in the institution.

An often-told story is the Tip O'Neil tale in which a freshman got an interview with Tip to ask for a plum committee assignment, to which Tip said, "Are you one of the new class of freshman? Go home and get re-elected so I can see if you are for real!"

Getting into the inner ring of the Speaker or the Chairman of your desired committee is one of the first tasks every member sets his or her mind to as the session begins. How do you pledge your fealty or vote to the Chairman? How do you show proof of your believability?

In 1993–1994, I was the leader of a Single-Payer Health Care caucus, and I had ninety-five pledged votes. Chairman Rostenkowski was moving toward bringing out a bill that he and Mrs. Clinton had crafted that was not a single-payer scheme. Danny, one day, drifted up to me on the floor, and said, "Doc, if we bring my bill to the floor without single-payer in it, will you support my bill?"

I knew the implications of opposing the Chairman and said, "I know the rules. You have my vote." I acquiesced for future consideration. He knew it, and I knew it. I was in the inner ring, and there was no benefit to opposing him, and thus, being on the outside. This is the normal way of operation in the circles and overlapping circles of the political process.

But C.S. Lewis told his audience the day will come when the request from a member of the circle is not quite right, and you will know it. Will it be a vote for a bad amendment or a request for silence in committee when an issue you understand is being discussed and you don't explain the truth to the committee because a colleague has asked you to be quiet? Or will it be an effort to word a contract so that it avoids scrutiny and is awarded to a friend?

A situation like that came up in the Ways and Means Committee one day. We had a bill before the committee for amendments, and as I read the bill, I noticed a provision that sounded like it was related to a legal case against Microsoft. Employees at Microsoft had brought a suit to stop the practice of hiring people to do jobs where they sat next to company employees doing the same job but without the same benefits for health and retirement. These "so-called" independent contractors were indistinguishable from employees. The court found in favor of the independent contractors in the legal action.

Microsoft, having lost in court, came to Congress to change the law, which the court had interpreted in the contractor's favor. In reading the bill, I spotted this and asked a question. I was told to be quiet. The amendment was pulled on that day. I don't know if it was changed somewhere else. Those quiet little actions happen all the time. You just have to ask yourself how mad you want to make a powerful employer in your Congressional district.

The slide downhill is hard to reverse. If you succeed, the next one is easier. If you fail, it is important to show you aren't "untrustworthy" and will try harder to succeed. And so, step by step, you descend into *scoundrelhood*. No one sets out to do this.

Michael Cohen never dreamed as he went to the office for ten years that he would lie to keep Donald Trump's approval and consequently wind up headed for the penitentiary. He knew, as he called more than 500 people to threaten them, that if he failed, he was in danger of being put outside the inner ring.

What is most intriguing, and baffling, is that the moral truth of the Lewis lecture is not new, and we as humans continue to ignore it. The story is as old as the story of the fall of Jericho. Judeo-Christian history tells us that God told the Israelites, thousands of years ago, that He would deliver Jericho into their hands. One caveat that He gave was that no one should take any of the booty of war for himself.

The attack on Jericho was a total success. The walls fell down. But one man, Achan, disobeyed and took some of the spoils of war. He put them under the floor of his tent.

A few days later God told the Israelites to go against the city of Ai. To their surprise they got whipped by the men of Ai. Joshua, the Israelite leader, asked God why they had been defeated. God said, "Someone in the camp has sinned." Joshua lined everybody up and found the guilty party. Achan was identified as the offender and he and his family were stoned to death and all his wealth was burned. The next time the Israelites went against Ai, they won decisively.

The message in my Sunday school class was clear, "Your sin will find you out." No scoundrel expects to be discovered. As each escapade goes unpunished, the next one is easier. One can only wonder how the Trump family views the future.

Before you dive into this book about what makes politicians tick, let's imagine that you just elected a new person to represent you in Congress. You've read the newspapers and watched television, so you have a general idea about what goes on in the Congress. The question that I want you to think about is this: What type of person have I elected? What will this person accomplish or leave as a legacy?

Does this congressman want to be rich? Or famous? Does this congressman have the personality and patience to pass important pieces of legislation? Or will this congressman merely show up to vote and cast hundreds of votes but be relatively anonymous?

Most people who run for office have reasons for running, but sometimes those reasons are not clear to the voter. Some candidates have a basic idea about some area of legislation they would like to impact, but many members have no agenda other than accumulating power and influence. They don't talk about it, and they would never admit it except under duress.

They follow the principle as it was laid out by George Washington Plunkett in Tammany Hall around the turn of the twentieth century.

Mr. Plunkett was a city councilman in New York who also ran a sand and gravel business. When once confronted about all the contracts that his gravel business had received from New York City, he replied, "I seen my opportunities, and I took 'em."

In his case, his opportunities led to a good deal of wealth derived from his business. But this could be said about members of Congress who see their opportunities legislatively and quickly capitalize on them. That ability to spot an opportunity and take advantage of it is not something that is taught to any member of a legislative body, but it is a reaction by members to their own inner drives, which are largely outside of their own consciousness.

Some politicians are bold, brash, and aggressive; others are ingratiating, polite, and seem to have an interest in other people. The saying, "What you see is what you get" is not necessarily true about politicians, and people are constantly confused when they find out that what they saw is not what they got.

Most of the frustration with politics as experienced by the public stems from the fact that they fail to understand the basic human drives that drive politicians. Amazing as it may seem, the very things that drive ordinary human beings drive politicians. Ordinary human beings try to get rich, others want to be respected in their church and in the community but have no desire to be famous. Some want to be powerful in the PTA, or the church, or the community council, and so they go to meetings endlessly. Their goal is to have recognition in the community, and have it understood that they are powerful and can make things happen. Sometimes this impulse to make things happen gets transformed into becoming a candidate for office.

So, every time you look at a political office-holder like a congressman, ask yourself what he or she is trying to accomplish. Try to figure out whether the goal is money, love, or power. If you can do that with a given politician, you not only understand the politician, but you can predict his or her future actions. If you look only at the surface behavior of a politician, you will be like a member of the audience watching a magician. The politician will misdirect your attention to what he or she wants you to see, not what's really going on.

You will rarely go wrong if you understand that what politicians do is, at its very core, all about themselves in almost all cases.

CAREERS

*Train up a child in the way he should go and
when he is old he will not depart from it.*

PROVERBS 22:6

E VERYONE IN LIFE CHOOSES a career. We begin
when we are children by dreaming about
what we would like to be when we grow up.
One of the games that was played when I was
young was a Parker Brothers board game called
Careers. The object of this game was to succeed
in your career by obtaining fame, happiness, and
money. Each player began the game by choosing
a mixture of stars, hearts, and dollars, equaling
sixty points. Your life goal was either to create a
mixture of the three categories, or if you prefer,
you could put all your eggs in one basket.

In this game, you achieved success by going
through various occupations such as college,
ecology, and big business. Each player decides,
as in real life, on his or her own success formula.

The first player to achieve or exceed his or her own success formula is the winner of the game. It is interesting to note that the list of occupations open to young minds does include politics. The career path is filled with many of the tribulations of political life: from early defeat to the ultimate success of winning a Nobel Peace Prize.

In the children's version of this game, stars stand for fame. As adults, stars stand for power, either visible or invisible. For children, hearts stand for love from people they know. For adults, love can be obtained from public adoration or from individual human beings. Of course dollars for children are just like dollars for adults.

A politician's career aligns pretty closely with this game. As citizens try to understand politicians and their behavior, they must keep in mind that politicians are just like everyone else. Citizens often make the mistake of thinking that politicians are somehow different from the rest of the public. With that misconception in mind, we often feel mystified by the behavior of politicians.

Politicians who enter into public life with the goal of making money at some time generally wind up in trouble. In fact, often they wind up going to prison. Trying to make money while being a public servant is a dangerous endeavor.

The life of the politician is too transparent to allow them to hide their attempts to enrich themselves. Filing financial disclosures, releasing income tax forms, and making side deals with friends and cronies offer enemies multiple opportunities to expose the greedy and corrupt politician.

The main reason that most men and women choose to go into politics is that they want the power to change something. For some, the issue that they want to change might be fairly small. For others, it could be a huge national or international problem that they want to tackle. Power in the political arena takes two different forms. One form of power is associated with celebrity, and this type of politician uses their celebrity to influence the course of events. The other form of power is associated with invisibility. The person in the political world who uses this form of power strives to have influence while never being seen. They try to operate behind the scenes so that they never expose themselves to public attack.

Senator Warren G. Magnuson (D-WA) used to say, "You have show horses and you have work horses. I don't like show horses."

Many of the work horses do not seek political office but operate as confidants, paid assistants, or as major contributors. While there are famous examples of elected politicians who were nearly invisible, they are the exceptions to the rule that public life does not allow invisibility. There are too many people involved for any serious politician to believe that what he or she has done will never come to light.

There is an interface between power and love that all politicians have to navigate. In order to get elected, one must be loved by at least fifty percent plus one of the constituents. Many successful politicians manage to be loved by seventy-five, eighty, or even ninety percent of their constituency. This requires a delicate dance between use of power on the one hand, and presenting an unattractive political persona on the other hand. Appearing to be too heavy-handed, vapid, or power-hungry is not an attractive political persona.

Politicians struggle eternally with trying to accumulate power on the one hand and appearing just like they're powerless on the other. Appearing too articulate or erudite can be much more dangerous than appearing to be bumbling and rumpled. In fact, many politicians try to emulate the less attractive aspects of their constituents' behavior. Especially during campaign seasons, the public is treated to pictures of politicians doing all sorts of things that they either would never do during the rest of their term or feel very uncomfortable doing unless it is part of a campaign appearance. If Brooks Brothers suits are your favorite form of attire, appearing in Levis and cowboy boots never seems to look right, and the public just laughs.

There is another form that love takes in the political process. Politicians, both men and women, are in contact with hundreds of people who have their own agenda. Seductive behavior is used both by politicians and some of their constituents. Because the contact between politicians and constituents is often fleeting and superficial, politicians frequently make mistakes, involving themselves in relationships that are not appealing on the front page of the newspaper. Again and again, the public opens the newspaper to find pictures of politicians involved with other human beings in a way that brings public condemnation.

One has to look at each situation in detail to diagnose whether or not the problematic relationship grew out of stupidity, arrogance, or a deep need to feel appreciated by some other human being. It is always clear that the politician involved thought he or she was clever enough to be invisible and that their partner really cared enough not to reveal the relationship to anyone else. It is a very rare relationship that is so secret that no one else knows about it.

One can say with almost total certainty that no politician has any chance of having such a relationship. Again and again, this desire for love leads politicians to make political mistakes.

In this era of television, the Internet, and social media, including YouTube, the intrusion of all private spaces in which politicians live is very widespread. Being continually on display and therefore being judged on all manner of superficialities is a chronic condition in which a politician lives. One must assume that one is always on display and that displays of affection or raw power will be captured in some form and later used in some negative way. Every microphone is hot; every telephone is a camera; and every reporter has the record button turned on.

Through this murky world, a politician struggles to increase his or her power without appearing brutal or crass, while at the same time trying to appear lovable to his or her constituency. The public recognizes this difficulty, almost unconsciously. It is expressed in phrases like, "I don't know how you do it. I couldn't stand it." Or sometimes they say, "don't you ever get tired of this. How do you get time for yourself?"

I've often joked with people that, like Richard Nixon and Jesus Christ, I'm a Capricorn. The Capricorn in the zodiac is often depicted as a mountain goat. The motto of the mountain goat is: "surefooted in high places." Behind the joke is the understanding that one false move or misstep can mean total disaster.

Although many readers of this book did not play the game of *Careers* as child, they have clearly played it as an adult. What were your goals? Did you want to be rich? Or did you just want enough money to be happy? Do you care what your neighbors think of you? Do you want to make things happen in your community or church or club or union hall? Those are the same questions which every politician faces every day. Only the scale or the breadth of our desire is different. The difference comes from the fact that what politicians do is done in full public view at all times. Politicians are like goldfish in a bowl. They are visible to anyone who cares to look This book is attempt to look behind caucus doors to share with you what really happens and how politicians fill out their careers.

MY RAISON D'ETRE
IN POLITICS

As I WATCH THE disintegration of the democ-racy under Donald Trump, I came to real-ize that my original framework for this book (as described in the previous chapter that politicians are motivated by love, money, and power) was deeply flawed. I had conceived of a book that would explore the changes people go through as they become members of the House of Represen-tatives. But truly, no one entering the Congress has any idea of the scope of issues they will face.

As this awareness dawns on me, I am reminded of the scene in the movie, *The Can-didate*, where Robert Redford admits to his campaign manager that he has no idea where he is going. As this awareness blossoms inside the newly elected public servant, he or she begins to feel the weight of his responsibility.

For any public servant, it is at this point that a whole new behavioral element begins to emerge. It is rarely explicitly discussed in much depth. But anyone who holds public office has an internal dialogue around the question, "Why am I here?"

Two types of people choose to run for office. The first group consists of those who want some combination of *money*, *love*, and *power*. As mentioned previously, they are the show horses. They want to be seen, acknowledged, admired, petted, and coddled. This group represents the majority of members of Congress.

The second (and smaller) group consists of those who wish do something for the community through public service. Most members in this group do not understand how a legislative body works, and they are often frustrated by its inefficiency and the endless process. They come to Congress to affect change based on ideology, religion, scientific, or work experiences. They are driven by a belief that something needs to change. These are the work horses. While these are two distinct types, there are clearly mixed breeds in the herd, and with these hybrid members, one has to look carefully to see which is the dominant trait.

For this book, I was in a quandary: Should I tell my tale from the beginning and show my evolution? Or, should begin at the end by looking at what I think I accomplished? I chose the former because that is how the story unfolds for any office holder.

All of this is preamble to my own tale. I never thought about a career in politics until I was enraged by the war in Vietnam. I ran for the Washington State Legislature in 1970 to end the Vietnam War. I had no idea what I was doing, but I was convinced that I was doing something.

I was approached to run for Congress at the end of my first term in the Washington State House by our Senator, Henry Jackson (D-WA), who was a hawk on the war. I was afraid I'd be controlled by him if he helped me win. For that reason, I ran for governor, thinking that being one of fifty governors gave me a better chance to influence the president to end the war. This was not an ego trip to "be someone." I had no idea what the governor of a state really did. I wanted access to talk to the president about my experience as a physician, taking care of the troops who came back from Vietnam. The war was still going unabated, and I was enraged by it. I was naïve.

That governor's race ended in humiliating defeat and debt, but I began looking for a way to mitigate what I saw as an evil in campaigns: money. I became the chair of a committee to defend the recently passed Initiative 276, which was a sunlight law on money being spent in state politics. My awareness of the complexity of politics was deepened quickly by that experience. It prepared me for my next move.

I was asked to run for the Washington State Senate. I had learned in my short stay in the House about the reach of the legislature in affecting the citizenry. I realized, by that time, that the reason I lost the governor's race was, at least in part, due to the fact I knew nothing about how the state ran. I felt like an intern who wants to do brain surgery but hasn't taken the time to do a residency. I ran for the Senate with the idea in mind that I might run for the governorship in two years.

Still learning, I found that that road was blocked by a constitutional provision that said you could not run for an office if the salary had been raised while you were in office. We had raised the governor's salary, which kept the field clear of any senators. So, I prepared to learn how state government worked. I served on multiple committees to gain knowledge. Over the next six years, I sat on about two-thirds of the committees in the Senate. Chairing the Education Committee, I wrote the Basic Education Law required by a Supreme Court decision, defining what was "ample education for all the children of the state."

I created a Special Nursing Reform Committee to look at reforming how our elderly were being cared for and how elder care was financed. I was denied the chair of this committee because I voted against the leadership on a procedural vote. When I complained, the majority leader simply said, "Don't ever vote against leadership on procedural votes." Another lesson for beginners. Leadership has a memory for past offenses. I had committed that offense six months before and forgotten it.

I sat on the Budget Committee, Ways and Means Committee, State Government and Local Government Committees, and I slowly learned how government was financed.

The year, 1976, was a year of turmoil across the whole country. After Nixon's resignation in 1974, the Democrats were looking for "non-political" politicians for candidates. A governor and peanut farmer of a southern state was chosen. Jimmy Carter, a novice to Washington, won the nomination and the presidency. He was a little better prepared than the college professor chosen by Richard Nixon to head the Atomic Energy Commission.

In 1976, Dixy Lee Ray (D-WA) was an affable biology professor from the University of Washington who made her reputation teaching oceanography on Public TV. In 1973, she was appointed by Nixon to be head of the Atomic Energy Commission. She also became a candidate for governor. The "Ocean Lady" was more acceptable to the voters than the more experienced and better known mayor of Seattle, and she won the governorship. During her four-year term, she successfully alienated her entire base and was ripe to be defeated.

In 1980, I was ready, and I knew my stuff. Unfortunately, the Speaker of the House, John Bagnariol (D-WA), was also ready. The Governor never saw me coming, but she was clearly afraid of the Speaker. She instituted a gambling sting against him, which led to charges in court and ultimately a conviction with a resulting two-year sentence.

With John Bagnariol out of the race in 1980, I won the primary by more than 250,000 votes, which were in large measure, Republicans who would switch back in the general election. The state was through with Dixy.

However, on the national scene, Ronald Reagan was running against President Jimmy Carter. Reagan was a skilled actor who used the slogan, "Let's Make America Great Again," which was later used by Donald Trump in 2016. The Republican National Committee sent a campaign operative to Seattle to help turn the tide against me back to John Spellman, the Republican nominee for Governor.

The operative's name was Joe Allbaugh. I met Joe when he was FEMA director for George

W Bush. He quietly told me, as we were viewing the damage caused by the earthquake in Seattle in 2001, that he was the one who came up with the TV ad campaign that beat me:

"DO YOU WANT A LIBERAL, SEATTLE PSYCHIATRIST TO BE YOUR NEXT GOVERNOR?"

Three strikes, and I was out.

I was beaten again, but this time not in debt, and I was still in the Senate. My family and I went to Kauai to lick our wounds. While we were absorbing the warmth of the sun in late December, I got a call from the Majority Leader, Ted Bottiger (D-WA), who had only been lukewarm in support for me. He was pals with Dixy, and he was looking for an appointment to a well-paying job to round out his pension. We were not close.

His phone call was to offer me the chairmanship of the Ways and Means Committee. We talked for a long time about what the next session would be like. I pointed out that we had a one vote majority in the Senate (25–24) and had lost the majority in the House. I knew all the members very well, having served with them for six years. I was worried about one particular member who had openly supported the Republican gubernatorial candidate, John Spellman. I told Ted that I needed every Democrat vote to do a balanced budget. He had to deliver everyone. I had no intention of failing again. He said, "What about Peter von Reichbauer (D-WA)?"

I replied, "if you can't get him to vote with us, I'll move to take the Transportation Committee from him the next time we are in Caucus." Ted was shocked and suggested I shouldn't do that. My reply was, "Don't try me."

The economy was bad and state revenues began falling. By February it was clear we would need to make some cuts to the budget so that we would not be in deficit in June. The only real place to make cuts in a state budget are in education and human services. Pensions and transportation are protected. Here is where my goals come to the foreground. I protected the poor and needy and cut education. Peter refused to vote for the budget. I told Ted, "Get his vote for the budget on Wednesday."

Peter voted on Wednesday, and the next day became a Republican, overturning everything in the Senate. Offices, committee chairs, staff. The Republicans got everything in terms of overt power symbols. Names on doors, parking spots, the works.

But I knew that knowledge is the real power. I knew the state budget was in big trouble and I knew that having the Governor's chair and the majorities in the House and Senate wouldn't magically fix it. I waited. Timing is everything.

One day, Jeanette Hayner, the Republican Majority Leader, came to me asking for some help in getting votes for their budget. She was three votes short. They were believers in Reagan, and Reagan had said, "No new taxes," and that was it for them. They were immovable. She was desperate. The Governor was no help. He had baited me about my stand on taxes, and I said, "I don't want to raise taxes but, if I think it is necessary, I'll propose them to the legislature." That finished me in the election.

But Hayner was a smart negotiator. She was opposed to raising property taxes, business taxes, and the state sales tax, so what was left? We had no income tax. We haggled about raising the business taxes, but finally she played her ace.

In 1979, by initiative, the seniors of the state took the sales tax off food. This was a huge loss of revenue to the state. She needed three votes from me to reinstate the sales tax on food. Nothing could have been more anathema to a liberal Democrat than this proposal, and she knew it. Rather than reject it, I said, "What will you give me to soothe my members' consciences at overturning the people's will?" I asked for almost all the cuts to be restored in the human services areas and even some adult dental benefits for people on public assistance.

Then my task was to get the votes of three Democrats who had districts that bordered on the Columbia river with Oregon. Many people in that area, as a matter of course, shop in Oregon because they have no sales tax. The restoration of the sales tax would have little or no effect on those members who voted for it. The bill passed and the budget was balanced.

Within a month, I filed Initiative 363 to remove the sales tax from food. I quickly got 400,000 signatures to the dismay of the Republicans. With the momentum of this citizen drive, we won both the Senate and House in the election of 1982. Jeanette said, "You didn't tell me you were going to do this." My answer was. "You never asked."

I still wanted to get universal health care. I started writing a bill called the Washington Basic Health Plan, which was a subsidized managed care plan designed by Group Health, our local healthcare cooperative. It had a sliding fee scale for people who were above the poverty line and not eligible for Medicaid. They couldn't buy individual coverage because they didn't have enough money. Waiters and waitresses, aspiring actors and actresses, artists, subsistence farmers, and many others would be eligible.

The election of 1984 was coming, and I planned to use Basic Health in my campaign. As Ways and Means chair, I did everything in my power to help the voting blocs I needed to win election: teachers, state employees, union workers, law enforcement, and firefighters.

The moment of truth came when I met with the Teachers Union and they said, "We can't support you. You are a two-time loser." Losing never helps your resume and most politicians try to avoid the experience.

I made another strategic error at this point. I knew I was better prepared and experienced in state government than my opponent, so I decided to run in spite of this ominous sign. A few weeks later in a debate before the Downtown Rotary Club in Seattle, I performed convincingly and felt like I could make a success of the campaign. That was Wednesday.

On Friday my opponent who happened to be a Weyerhaeuser heir, sat down and wrote a check to purchase every good available TV ad slot until the primary election. I was dead again. I had some campaign advertising, but I lost.

After the campaign I met with the new governor and told him I would do everything I could to help make his administration succeed. He signed the Washington Basic Health Act into law, and I helped him fund the Puget Sound cleanup. But his staff never trusted me, and they kept trying to undercut what I was doing in the Legislature.

One day the Governor appointed the Majority Leader to a well-paying commission so he could get a sizable pension. I decided to run for Majority Leader, but no one would give me their vote. I confronted one of them and said, "Frank, do you remember all the stuff I've done for you? Can you tell me why you won't help me in this Majority Leader's race?"

Frank said, "You have been a fabulous Ways and Means chair, and we want you to stay there. If you got to be Leader, you'd make us do things we don't want to do."

I knew I'd hit the ceiling in the Legislature, and I was going to have lots of problems advancing my health and human services agenda. So, I quit politics and went back to medicine. I took a job as a regional psychiatrist for the State Department. I threw all my political fundraising records in the dumpster and left for Kinshasa, Zaire. I hit a wall. I had two kids in college and no stable practice, so I needed income to support my family. I saw no political future. All our Federal jobs were held by good politicians.

And then Senator Henry Jackson died, and all the political cards were reshuffled. My brother and my campaign manager called and said, "You must come home. We have just the seat for you to pursue to get National Health insurance." I listened and said, "No. I have a stable life finally and my kids are being educated. I've learned all you can learn from losing. Two of my friends are already candidates, a woman and a black city councilman. Why would Seattle elect another good old white boy to the Congress?" But they had sunk the hook in my desire to do something, namely get a universal single payer health care system in place.

The rest is twenty-eight years of Congressional history, trying to get a bill passed. I lived through the Clinton years, and we failed, but I got wiser. When Obama appeared on the scene, he quickly made it clear that single payer was not his goal. He had made his deal with big insurance and big pharma, and I tried to make changes allowing a public option, but I couldn't get it out of the House. Luckily, Senator Cantwell (D-WA) got a public option like the Washington Basic Health Plan into to the text of Obamacare.

Obamacare was not perfect and didn't fix all the problems, but it was a start. I worked on that issue for almost forty-five years. We tried for several years to complete what our country needs, but the forces from industry were too strong and have diminished the President's program. They may, in the future, complete the dismantling.

I met Jay Rockefeller shortly before I left Congress. Jay was a work horse, not a show horse, and he told me he, too, was retiring. "Jim, I'm on boards of corporation that have seventy-year-old mandatory retirement. You and I are eighty. Let's let the young and eager ones finish our work."

My *raison d'etre* in politics was to try to make health care available for all people. I did lots of other things for the environment, children's and veteran's issues, trade with Africa, the AIDS pandemic, and on and on. But I kept coming back. My last effort as I left Congress was to get eyeglasses and hearing aids included in Medicare. Since I left, it seems it has passed.

COMMEMORATIVES

A FORMER STAFFER OF mine told me a story that underscores one of the dilemmas for every member of Congress. My friend went to the window in the post office to buy some postage stamps. She asked to see what commemoratives were available. The young postal clerk looked at her with a sincere face and said, "What's a commemorative?"

Every member of Congress comes to the Congress wanting to be remembered; essentially, they want to be commemorated for something or some group of things that they have accomplished. I'm sure every representative arrives as I did with some laudable goal in mind. I wanted to establish a national health insurance plan. Others came wishing to make changes in environmental protection or advances in labor law or gender equality.

Through the process of creating legislation, every member hopes to do something that will be commemorated when they retire from the Congress. While working on these weighty pieces of legislation, one discovers that it's not as easy or as quick to accomplish anything as was originally imagined. Every member who has worked on a project can tell you how many years it took to get it through the Congress. Changes of leadership in committees or in the party leadership all play a part in slowing the process down to the point where it is hard to tell if any progress is ever made.

Meanwhile, every representative receives thousands of letters, emails, and phone calls with requests for various types of help. Difficulties with foreign adoptions, funding for a building project, admission to a military academy, or a search for some war medal that had been awarded to a relative dating back to 1918. These issues had all been the subject of requests to my office. The staff called it casework, and it was work indeed, figuring out where in the bureaucracy progress is (or will be) halted on a given request.

Many of these episodes stick in my mind. One of the most dramatic and earliest in my career taught me a very important lesson. One of my precinct committeemen had diabetes, and as a result, he had lost his lower leg to infection. He had been fitted for a prosthetic device, but it never came. He was on Medicaid, so he called his elected official, me, and I set about to find out what happened. I called the secretary of Health and Human Services and left a message. The next day, I got a message from the secretary saying that he found my request on the top of his inbox, and the man in question would receive his artificial limb within a few days. A few days later our office received a phone call from the man, proclaiming, "There's a been a miracle. My leg came today!" He had been waiting for four months. He told everyone in his political organization that I was a miracle worker. I had his vote and all his friends' votes for as long as I stayed in political office.

Any member of Congress or public official can tell you hundreds of stories like this. What they don't tell you is that the people you help remember you even after you are out of office. I've been retired now for about four years, and I continue to meet people who tell me about things that my office did for them as far back as thirty years ago. In 2016, one of the last meetings I had in my office before I left was with employees of a labor union. This union represents maintenance workers and janitors, of which many of the members come from Central or South America. Before the meeting started, one of the men stood up and said, "I want to say something." He proceeded then, to thank me for a call I made in 1991 to the embassy in San Salvador, El Salvador. After my call, he said, the authorities opened the gates of the local prison and let him out. He emigrated to the United States, became a citizen, and was now a union official for his labor union. More on El Salvador later.

The truth is, I did not know the effect of my phone call. In most cases, I never knew. My staff was doing the work that led to these "miracles." Since my retirement, as I walk around in my district, I continue to meet people who remind me of things that my office did for them over the years.

For members of Congress who want to be loved by their constituents, the best way is to do something for voters that they actually asked for, and need. Some members routinely ignore the requests of their constituents, and they often find themselves in difficulty at election time because people who have been disregarded often get angry. This lack of responsiveness cost a congressman in Washington several hundred thousand dollars of his own money to salvage a campaign because he never read and answered his constituent letters. He won by a few votes and retired the next term.

If you want to be commemorated, help your people. Very few members are remembered for a piece of legislation that they helped to pass. But voters never forget when the member actually listens to their problems and makes an effort to provide solutions.

When you retire from Congress, you become a celebrity of sorts. You survived politics for a lot of years, so you must know the secrets to success. Not long after I retired, I began getting requests for interviews from medical students and doctors to talk about how I entered into politics and how my training helped me in politics. As the Trump catastrophe folded into the COVID-19 epidemic, the calls increased. The questions made me think about my medical training, and how I used it on a regular basis.

Dr. William Osler from Johns Hopkins Medical School, who is often called the father of American Medicine, is reported to have said to a class in the late 1890s, "Listen to the patient. He or she is telling you what is the matter with them."

This advice is as valid today as it was 125 years ago. Put more bluntly, ask the question and then, "Shut up!"

My favorite example of the situation is exemplified by a doctor friend named Bob Putsch.

He was from Montana and trained in infectious disease. He joined the US Public Health Service (USPHS) and was assigned to the Navaho Reservation in the Four Corners region of the west. He spent three or four years there and really came to understand Native American thinking about western medicine. When he left the reservation, he worked in community clinics in Seattle, where there was a multiplicity of ethnic groups from Asia, Africa, and Central and South America. His skill, honed by experience in Arizona and New Mexico, became well known as he worked the wards at the USPHS hospital in Seattle.

His technique was simple. When he was asked to see a puzzling patient, he would grab a chair, take the patient's hand, sit down, and then ask, "Tell me why you think you are sick?" He would listen to the explanation of the cause of the ailment. He never corrected their understanding of the science of western medicine. He simply contrived a way to help them understand how western medicine might help to alleviate the hex, spell, or bad dream the patient thought was the cause.

As a congressman, I learned early that telling people what the solution was before they had a chance to have their say was not helpful. They would invariably go away saying, "He didn't listen to me."

My staff would cringe when I was in a hurry and greeted a group by saying, "Well what do you want today?" I tried to be more diplomatic in most cases but sometimes cutting to the chase worked better. My staff also told me that I listened too long to people who couldn't or wouldn't understand. In psychiatry, I learned an old aphorism that claimed, "a schizophrenic patient was like a stopped clock. Your job was to find out what time it stopped, so keep listening."

In politics, I listened to many interesting theories about why certain events occurred or might occur. Often as I listened, I thought about how I might help. I can only remember one time when I refused to listen.

Early in my career I was active with the peace community in Seattle. A young woman from my church, St. Mark's Cathedral, had been working in San Salvador, El Salvador. She and her boyfriend were living together in a house that was raided by the forces of the dictator, Alfredo Christiani. Weapons were found in the front yard of her house. I was at a Thanksgiving family gathering on Lopez Island in Washington State. My peace friends insisted that I should go down to El Salvador and use my influence to protect her.

I flew down that day. The next day, I saw her in the prison. She started to tell me her story, and

I stopped her by saying, "If you keep quiet and don't say another word to me or any seemingly friendly person, we will get you out. You can't trust anyone you don't know, and you never know who is listening." A week later, Ramsey Clark, Lyndon Johnson's former Attorney General, negotiated her deportation back to the United States. Jennifer Casolo was the only person I can remember to whom I deliberately told not to tell me her story.

Politicians sometimes offer solutions to problems constituents are not ready to deal with at the time. Proposing solutions at such a time leads to frustration on both sides. If you listen like Bob Putsch, you will often think of a way to propose or phrase a proposal that will make the constituent willing to accept. Getting a patient who thinks they have a hex on them to take four pink tablets twice a day takes thoughtful patience and skillful delivery of the message.

Politicians who listen and solve problems for people are never forgotten. If you are an elected official who listens, you can help numerous people, many of whom you will never know. As I respond to these requests for mentoring, I have begun thinking of dozens of acts, large and small, that have helped people whose names I have forgotten. What you remember are the events that you caused to occur.

The interesting thing about listening and then proposing or initiating a solution is that, as a politician, you do something and move on to the next issue. You seldom have time to review all that you have done because there is always a new set of problems.

Here is another example: The Hubble Telescope was damaged during construction and needed repairs, but the decision was made by NASA to let the telescope die and invest in the Webb Scope that was planned to be launched in the near future. This was in the 1990s.

At that time, I got a call from a fifth grade school teacher in a school outside my district. She wanted to show me what the students were doing with Hubble Telescope data. I showed up to her class and saw thirty enthusiastic children counting galaxies and stars off of Hubble photographs. They were learning about solar systems and stars I knew very little about at fifty-five years old. But it was clear that letting the scope die was a bad idea.

I went back to Congress the next week and talked to Mark and Tom Udall about the subject. I don't remember what directed me to them, but together we made a push in the Appropriations Committee to get the repair project funded. The result of that effort is that the Hubble telescope is still sending magnificent pictures back to earth, and the Webb Space telescope will not be commissioned any earlier than October, 2021. If you look at the NASA site on Google, you will find that the Hubble Telescope has been repaired several times, and it is the greatest telescope ever developed. And it was saved in part by a fifth grade teacher calling a Congressman who listened. My staff me told me I shouldn't get involved because the school was in the adjoining Congressional district represented by a Republican. Staff is always cautious, but it is never wrong to listens to others.

THINK BEFORE YOU LEAP

IF YOU'RE A CITIZEN thinking of running for Congress, the question you should ask yourself is this: "Are you ready to get up every morning at 6:00 A.M. to begin cold calls to Washington lobbyists to beg for money?" Unless you're rich and can pay for your own campaign, you are going to become a shameless beggar. Citizens should know that the minute a representative is sworn in, he or she must start raising money for re-election.

American politics is dominated by money. I don't mean influenced by money; I mean dominated. If something doesn't make sense to you in the political scene, follow the French maxim: *Cherche l'argent*. You can better understand why something doesn't add up if you find the source of money and its effects. This isn't easy. It is often convoluted or hard to trace.

Your representative cannot hide efforts to raise money unless he or she wants to spend time in prison. Campaign finance laws force transparency. However, these laws do not cover all bad behavior, such as an immediate request for attendance to the next fundraiser to anyone who was granted an audience with the member. This type of abuse is hard to prove, but more than one lobbyist told me of offices where this was standard practice. Now with email, the request to attend the next fundraiser often beats the lobbyists back to their offices. This isn't illegal, but it does have the stench of the swamp.

When a candidate starts a race, rarely does he or she think about campaign finance laws. I was a rarity because I had been the Washington State Chairman of the Coalition for Open Government in 1973, which produced our campaign disclosure law. I, at least in theory, knew the rules. By the time I ran for Congress, I had run three times for governor, four times for the state Senate, and once for the state House of Representatives. So, I was experienced at minor league politics and fundraising. In that time, I'd seen the Washington State Senate Majority Leader go to prison for two years because he failed to report a $43 in-kind contribution of a clipping service in a race for attorney general. The contribution was part of a sting operation by the governor against a potential rival for her re-election to the governorship. My colleague went to prison, and I got the gubernatorial nomination.

With all this background, I began my campaign for Congress. I was fifty-one years old, had two kids in college, and an interesting job in Africa with the State Department. I was in a contest against two other candidates, a woman who was the county assessor, and an African American city councilman. I knew I would need money for TV ads in this race. They were both friends of mine, and they had campaigns up and running from races that they had just finished successfully. I was coming back from Africa to take them on.

When I left the Washington State Senate, I threw away all my fundraising lists. I was done with politics. I had to start all over again raising money. I was scared because I had lost three races for governor, and I knew how central money was to winning this district.

For three months I called potential donors almost continuously. I didn't spend on staff or brochures or any campaign paraphernalia. All the money went into an account for TV ads. It was grueling and mind deadening to try for five hours to convince Washington lobbyists and old friends to give. Some knew me and some didn't, but like a baseball pitcher on the mound, you must keep your concentration and throw the ball in the strike zone.

No one is as good as the candidate at raising money. If the candidate asks, a link is made between the donor and the candidate. The bond goes both ways. The donor, once having contributed, wants his horse to win and tells his friends. The candidate feels in debt to the contributor. A lobbyist once said to me, "If you can't eat my steak and drink my wine and then vote against me, get out of this game. You will never have any integrity if you can't." Despite that great philosophy, any honest officeholder knows when he or she is voting for something that is going to break the bond with a contributor.

Small contributors expect little beyond honest representation, but large donors expect something in return. If you ask them, they will deny it. Often a member who has done the hard work of raising money, when confronted with a vote on some issue will say to himself, "If I vote for that, I'll lose my next election." That is short-hand for, "I took money from these people, and I can't go against them."

The alternative to raising money from lobbyists is to raise money from grass roots supporters. This is a constant project to raise small amounts of money from large numbers of people. I won my elections with 200,000 people voting for me and I tried to get them to contribute $10 each. That would have grossed $2,000,000, but the organization to achieve that goal would have been enormous. Now, candidates flood my email inbox with numerous requests per day. On a given day, I get at least sixty requests for small donations. Most people do not respond. People are now awed by the substantial monthly contribution numbers raised through grass roots campaigning and can't believe that all of these small donations can change things.

And by the way, it never gets easier. When I came to Congress, I arrived with Nancy Pelosi (D-CA) and Peter Hoagland (D-NE). We were all on the Banking Committee during the Savings and Loan crisis of 1989, and we sat through day-long hearings for weeks on the causes of the financial debacle. In the afternoon sessions, Nancy and I noticed that Peter, a Harvard trained lawyer, was never there. I asked him where he was.

He said," I arrived in Washington, $500,000 in debt, and I have to raise that and then start raising the $1,000,000 for the next race. He lasted three terms and then was beaten in the Gingrich sweep of 1994 by a guy married to the daughter of a Florida millionaire. An interesting story came out of this race. Under Democratic chairmen of the Ways and Means Committee, no freshman ever got on the Committee in their first term. The Committee chair insisted on the right to watch a new member to see if he or she could be counted on to follow the Chairman's lead. In 1995, as the Gingrich sweep came in, the freshman from Omaha who replaced Peter Hoagland suddenly flew into Washington on his father-in-law's jet and was instantly on the Ways and Means Committee. A true miracle. The rumor was that significant money was contributed by the father-in-law, and a seat was purchased on the Committee.

When I came into Congress in 1989, everyone raised his or her own campaign funds. By 1994 under Nancy Pelosi, the Democratic Caucus Campaign Committee became the center of fundraising as we moved forward. They set up an office and phones and members began to go there to raise money. Newt Gingrich (R-GA) set fundraising goals that he demanded that Republicans members meet. There is no difference between the parties in this respect.

Today the Democrats follow the same program. As a senior member of our Caucus, I was expected to raise $250,000. In 2014, I managed to raise about $214,000. Two of the Democrats on the Ways and Means Committee raised the objection that I should not be Chairman of the Health Subcommittee since I had not raised my Caucus dues. I pledged to do better in the next cycle. I was not a good fundraiser despite trying to do my part. I was told by donors, big and small, that I had a safe district and didn't need money. To be honest, I could never bring myself to tell people I needed money to pay my dues to the Caucus.

There is a rough justice in life. I decided to leave Congress when it became clear to me that the financial interests of the country didn't want me to succeed Sandy Levin (D-MI), who was a left leaning Chairman of the Ways and Means Committee. I was next in seniority, and I was followed by John Lewis (D-GA), an icon of probity in the body. The moneyed interests of the country wanted a more flexible chairman who would both listen them to and do what they wanted. My accusers on the Ways and Means Committee had an interesting year following my departure. One was defeated by an insurgent in his own primary, and the other, who served on the Ethics Committee, had an ethics charge filed against her husband.

As you watch how your representative votes, consider how costly it is to win a seat in Congress and who helped put your representative there.

PUBLIC SERVICE

To understand a politician, you must understand the experience he or she went through to become an elected official.

Every politician remembers in great detail the first race they ran and won. The harrowing experience of going from private life into the political arena is a life-changing experience. Politicians all speak longingly of the private life they left with great nostalgia. Time for yourself and family away from the prying eyes of the public is remembered fondly. But it is the rare politician who purposely chooses to leave public life and return to private life.

The new landscape of public life is filled with excitement, challenge, and endless terror. The drive for money, love, and power is very alluring, and the chance to make something happen is intoxicating.

While I was in the US Navy at Long Beach during the Vietnam War, I thought about how

I wanted to get into politics to stop the war. I wanted to run for Congress in 1970, even though I had only lived in Washington State for two years, from 1966 to 1968, and thus I had no political base whatsoever. The few friends I had encouraged me not to run for Congress, but instead to run for the Washington State Legislature. How was I to know that I lived in the 43rd District in the State of Washington, a district that had never in eighty-one years elected a Democrat to the state legislature. Being full of energy and confidence, I launched a campaign, believing if I worked hard and talked to the people, I would earn their vote.

During my two years in the Navy, I met a young legal officer from Virginia named Russell Robertson. He had been Sam Rayburn's (D-TX) personal page in the House Representatives, and he had been involved in Virginia politics for much of his adult life. He and I made a pact that the first one who ran for office could call upon the other to help in the campaign. So, I called Russell.

Imagine a campaign run by an ambitious ignorant psychiatrist as the candidate and a slow drawling Virginian as the campaign manager. He was smart. He led me through the campaign, and I won. The problem was I thought I knew why I won. The fact was I didn't know anything. There were forces at work in my district about which I knew nothing at all. The district had always been represented by moderate Republicans, and my opponent on the Republican side was a very conservative Republican. My campaign was designed not to scare moderate Republicans away. It was the only time I ever ran as Dr. Jim McDermott. I've never used my medical degree in a prominent role in any of my campaigns, but in that first race it served the purpose of making me seem moderate. The moderate Republican governor that we had at that time was named Dan Evans. I ran as an Evans Democrat. I arrived in the state capital, Olympia, with lots of confidence and no knowledge about government or its inner workings. I suspect I made every possible beginners mistake. But I undoubtedly showed the great promise of rookies in every profession. The Republican Attorney General tried to get me to change my party affiliation. He was sure I'd feel more comfortable in the Republican Party.

Others told me I talked on too many things, and they counseled me to be more selective. They suggested that I picked several issues, become an expert on those issues, and remain silent the rest of the time. Whatever my performance might have been during that first session, I did well enough, and I was asked by Senator Henry Jackson to run for the US House Representatives. Jackson was a hawk on the war, and I detested him for it. I was afraid that if I ran for Congress I would be considered Henry Jackson's boy, and I could not tolerate that thought. I listen to other people who talked me into a run for the governorship of Washington State.

I ran for governor believing that if I worked hard and talked to people, I would win. I rode a bicycle more than 700 miles from Bellingham to Vancouver, Washington, but I did not do any serious fundraising. I ignored the advice of those who told me I would have to raise money to be a serious candidate. On election day, in the primary, I got seventeen percent of the Democratic vote. My career was at an end. I had no job. I was $8,000 in debt, and I didn't get to Congress until sixteen years later in 1988.

There is much more to the story, but every politician has a similar story to tell. To understand what drives politicians, one must understand what makes a person emigrate from the land of private life to the world of public life. Many politicians came from nothing; others came from great wealth. Some are well-educated; some have not had the benefit of a good education. Some politicians come as insiders with family connections; others come out of nowhere but figure out how to climb the ladder of political success.

There's a story from Chicago politics about the young man who went into City Hall, asking for a job. The person he met with said, "Who sent you?" The young man said, "No one sent me." The interviewer said, "Get out of here. We don't want nobody whom nobody sent."

No one can hope to understand politicians without looking into the details of how and why he or she came to the land of public life. To understanding a politician's actions, any serious student of the political process must understand the background from which the politician came.

FOR THE LOVE OF MONEY

For the love of money is the root of all evil:
which while some coveted after, they have
erred from the faith, and pierced themselves
through with many sorrows.

1 TIMOTHY 6:10

A BOOK ABOUT POLITICS cannot be taken seriously unless it has a lengthy discussion of the place of money at the heart of the system. Most people enter politics determined to make a change in the world around them. Some crisis or issue has driven them from the general population to the actions necessary to get elected. Their minds are filled with visions of what they will accomplish. For the new candidate, and for the voting public, the practicalities of politics are largely unknown, and the most dominant of those "practicalities" is money.

There are two types of money in politics: The first is the money you must raise to run a campaign. The second is the money you get for yourself and your family from holding public office. Let me begin with the fundraising for a campaign.

Very early on in my career, I decided to run for governor. A wily old pol who had been the chief of staff to an especially important Senator suggested to me, when I ask him for a donation, that I should go out and raise $25,000. After I had done that, I should come back to him. I laughed to myself at the time thinking he was a cynical politician who had lost all his values.

This was 1972, and it took me almost six months to raise $25,000. I was winning debates, and I was certain that people would elect me because of my ideas and my character. When the primary election came, my two opponents blew past me like runaway freight trains, using radio and television to inundate the population with messages about their superiority. I got seventeen percent of the vote in a primary election.

I ran for governor two more times, and I raised considerable amounts of money, but I met an opponent who could outspend me. In 1984, my opponent and I debated, and I trounced him. The next day, he sat down and wrote a $500,000 check, buying advertising that buried me alive. I lost that election too. I've often joked that I learned everything that one can learn from losing, and that was the rudest of all the lessons I've learned.

Since that time, I have not lost an election because I raise enough money to advertise for myself. I hated every minute I spent sitting at the phone calling people and begging for money. In 1987, I decided that I would never be elected to statewide office in Washington State. I had lost three gubernatorial elections, and there was no future in waiting for someone to die to open up a Federal office, so I joined the Foreign Service as a medical officer and headed for Zaire. Before I left, I took two pickup loads of political records to the dump. I threw away every single piece of political fundraising material.

In early 1988, my brother, and my campaign manager, called me to encourage me to come home from Africa and run for the United States Congress. I told them that I had kicked the habit of politics, and that I had no intention of ever returning to the political arena. Together they flew to Kinshasa, Zaire, to convince me that I could win this race. I told them I had a job I liked, and I didn't like the possibility that I would come home, having given up the job, and then lose the race. I had two kids in college, and if I lost, I didn't know how I could help them get an education. They assured me that I could win. I told them to go home, do an honest poll, and get $30,000 in commitments. They did it, and the rest is history.

I came home with no fundraising lists into a race where two of my Democratic friends were already running full tilt. Every morning at six o'clock, I got on the phone and called Washington, D.C., making cold calls to lobbyists from every imaginable industry. I refused to buy campaign merchandise until we had $300,000 in the bank, earmarked for the television commercials we would need for the weeks before the primary. Raising money in a Democratic district in a contested Democratic primary is a hard sell. People said to me, "How can we lose? Why should we waste our money in the primary? Call us in the general election when you need the money." I won the primary, but I hardly needed their money in the general election. I won the general by eighty-eight percent.

After I was in Congress for a few years, members of the Washington State Legislature or other interested parties would come to me for advice about running for the United States Congress. I had a three-point checklist of questions that must be answered. First, how old are your children and where are they going to live? Second, what is the worst thing you've ever done, and how would you feel if it became public knowledge? How would you explain it to the *Seattle Times*? Third, can you sit down tomorrow (and every other day that follows) and start raising money? I spent a lot of time raising money because it is the hardest reality that a politician faces. And this is important for citizens to know. Your representative is going to spend most of his or her time raising money. The only way your representative avoids this political necessity is to be wealthy and willing to pay for a campaign from personal wealth.

I always close my advice to aspiring candidates on the issue of money by telling them that if their campaign disclosure reports do not show significant money, no one will take them seriously, no matter how intelligent, attractive, or articulate they may be.

In a strange way this process is the reverse of the story that appears in *Luke 18:23* in the *New Testament*. In this story, a wealthy young man comes to Christ and asks, "How may he get into heaven?" Christ tells him to go and sell all that he has and give it to the poor. The story reports that the young man went away unhappy. Christ then observed that it is easier for a camel to go through the eye of a needle than it is for a rich man to get into heaven. The political equivalent to Christ's observation is that it is easier for camel to go through the eye of a needle than it is for a poor man to get in the Congress.

I once had a colleague in the Washington State Legislature named Frank Warnke (D-WA). Frank was a wily old union leader who had run many campaigns. He came up with a new idea which he ran by me. He told me that he was going to sell shares in himself, and that if you own a share of him, you would be allowed to make requests from him. Frank was the most honest fundraiser I ever met.

Campaign finance is one of the most corrupting aspects of the political system. Many bright and able people enter the political scene full of great visions and honest hearts. Almost to a person, I think, they believe that they do not have a price, and that they are accepting money without any obligation. That belief system comes crashing down when they run for office the second time. Very often they are stunned to find that people who gave money to them in the beginning will no longer support them. Some vote or some action or some failure of action turns their contributors against them. The representative must assess what each contribution means and what is expected by the contributor. With rare exceptions, the larger the contribution, the more is expected. Those who give small amounts want to participate, but they generally do not demand that their contributions be recognized by the candidate. Large organizational donations are very clearly tied to performance in the Congress.

Almost every representative is constantly calculating the impact of their votes on their contributors. They may tell you that they're thinking about their constituents, but if you could read their minds, they are thinking about where the money is going to come from for the next campaign. The cost of campaigns is beyond belief, and many good people do not venture into politics because they do not want to go through the soul searing process of raising money. My deepest fear is that the corporatization of politics will destroy our democracy. As campaigns become more and more expensive, the power of big money grows exponentially and its influence on the actions of Congress become the primary driver.

When I came to Congress, the process was done mostly by setting up a fundraiser and then inviting folks to come with money, giving them access to the candidate for a passing moment. Campaigns were relatively cheap then. Today, the costs are out of sight. Given that, the process has changed. The pressure is on. Both sides of the aisle have dollar amounts that are expected to be contributed to the caucus campaign committee. In the Democratic Caucus, I was expected to produce $250,000 due to my rank in the caucus. But my district doesn't give me big donations because I have a safe seat.

I am the ranking member on the health sub-committee. This is the top seat on the Ways and Means Committee for health related affairs, mostly Medicare. In 2014, I only raised a lit-tle over $200,000 and when the committee met to organize, I was challenged because I had not paid my dues. I promised I'd try harder next time, but that was the last straw for me. I refused to use the tried and true method of fundraising, which I have watched for twenty-eight years. It works like this. If you want an appointment with me, I look over my contributors list. If you aren't on the list, I won't see you. You will see staff. But I will give you a reprieve if you attend my next fundraiser and pay $1000 or more. It is called pay to play.

The stories are endless and appalling. One lobbyist told me of a visit to the Republican Majority Leader's office. Two wealthy citizens and two lobbyists asked to see the chief of staff. He appeared and said, "Have you contributed?" One citizen said "Yes, we have." The chief of staff said, "Under what name?" The citizen said, "Under my father's name or from the founda-tion that I run." The chief of staff said, "Wait a minute." The group watched him go to his gov-ernment computer. In a moment he returned and said, "Yes, you have. What can I do for you?" Very efficient, and very illegal! But it happens more than you want to know. I know one of the lobbyists who was there.

In the book of Mark in the *New Testament*, Christ asks the question, "What shall it profit a man if he gains the whole world and loses his own soul? Or what shall he give in exchange for his soul?"

LIVING THE HIGH LIFE

WHEN ORDINARY HUMAN BEINGS run for the House of Representatives, they have absolutely no idea what they're getting into. They see the Capitol Dome and have an idealized understanding of what it's like to serve in the United States Congress.

We had one representative from Washington State who declared that he would never take a salary increase because he felt the salary was sufficient for anybody serving in Congress. Shortly after he arrived here, he was seen at a reception and the question was asked, "How is it going?" He said, "It's terrible. I never realized how expensive it was to live in Washington, D.C., while I maintain a house back in Washington State."

When I came to Congress in 1989, the salary was $80,000 year. To maintain two houses 2300 miles apart turned out to be an expensive proposition. One weekend when I returned home to Seattle, the weather dropped in temperature to below zero in Washington, D.C. The pipes in my house were not insulated. The pipes froze, leaking water into the ceiling of the second floor bedroom. The ceiling came down on my bed, flooding the floor and warped floor. The water continued to soak through the floor and into the ceiling of the first floor dining room. The ceiling came down and that floor was warped.

My house had to be almost entirely rebuilt including ceilings and floors in two major rooms. Luckily my insurance company paid for the bulk of it. The difficulties of maintaining two houses is something that most members don't think about in advance.

Few people prepare for this very difficult area before they run for office. Before the advent of the Boeing 707, travel across the country was done once or maybe twice a year. Members of Congress brought their families with them to Washington, D.C., and they went home in August to avoid the heat. They returned in the fall, if necessary. Airline travel made it possible for people to travel home each week if they wanted to try to keep in touch with constituents.

In 1994 when Newt Gingrich won control of the House, he told his members to leave their families at home and come to Washington only when the Congress was in session. This produced a large number of unattached men

and women in Washington, D.C. The resulting entanglements are all over the newspaper.
The survival of marriage for a Congressman or
Congresswoman is always in doubt. If there's
trouble in the marriage, it is magnified by this
arrangement.

When I came to Congress in 1989, representatives bought houses. Today, unless you are
very well financed, buying a house is out of the
question. Most members live in rented spaces
with other members, so the concept of bringing your family or spouse to Washington, D.C.,
is an impossibility. Currently, there are about
sixty members living in their offices on a permanent basis. Futons, inflatable beds, and other
arrangements are the order of the day.

If you're thinking about sending your kids to
college, you have to save at every turn. Living in
your office is just one of the sacrifices that new
members make. In addition to living in your
office, the next problem is where are you going
to eat? Since you don't have an apartment to
keep or cook food, members eat out on a regular basis. Large dinners put on by organizations,
grazing at party dinners, or getting takeout is
very common. A home-cooked meal is a rarity.
One result of all of that is weight gain. Alcohol
consumption adds to the problems of people
who are eating irregularly by themselves.

Beginning with the era of Gingrich, the self-hate of people in Congress grew in many directions. There had been a negotiated salary increase limited to cost-of-living increases. Seven or eight years ago, the house voted not to take a salary increase. House salaries have been frozen since that time. Obviously, goods and services have risen in price, but members of Congress determined that they were not entitled to any salary increase.

In addition, the gymnasium, which used to be free, now costs $350 a year. They also added the cost of using the capital physician, which is now priced at $650 a year. This Congress would never think of charging federal employees like the military for using the gym to keep fit, but they punish themselves by charging themselves for this activity.

When I was in the State Department and the United States Navy as a federal employee, my health care was taken care of by the government. You might expect that the public would expect a healthy Congress doing their business. We expect the same from the Foreign Service and the military, but somehow the Congress punishes themselves by not providing the service. It is thought of as a perk.

Consider the problems of any member of Congress who has health issues. They have physicians in two different places. Miscommunication or lack of communication is very easy to understand. Getting appointments in Washington, D.C., or the hometown of the congressman is never easy and sometimes simply impossible. Since I've been in Congress, there have been at least one hundred different doctors in the capital physician's office. To get coordinated care from such a system is very difficult, especially when you throw in the complications of integrating care from back home.

People ask me about the plane flights and how difficult it is to return home. I usually reply, "I knew where the capital was when I asked for the job, and I knew that I'd have to travel back and forth, and I can quit this job any day I want, so why complain."

But if you ask any member of Congress about their experiences with airlines, they can give you a litany of problems that will run on for some time. People back home don't understand why you don't arrive when you said you would. It's especially hard on kids to expect a parent home at a certain time, and then it doesn't work out.

There was a time when Washington, D.C., was run by the Congress. Some call that the "plantation time." It was run as an absentee landlord might run it. The advent of home rule has brought more complications. The cabs in

Washington, D.C., were paid on the basis of what zone you were taken to. The rates were kept low and most members used their car very little. Cabs were readily available and moderately priced. That ended with home rule. Trying to get through the traffic of Washington, D.C., from an appointment downtown on K Street to the Capitol for a vote is nearly impossible. Parking downtown is expensive and hard to find. Free parking spaces are all but eliminated. Washington, D.C., raises a huge amount of its revenue from traffic and parking fines. Police cruise through neighborhoods at five o'clock in the morning to see if every car has a properly purchased zone permit for parking. Hundred dollar fines are regular occurrences. God forbid, you should be in your district when a snow comes and your car is parked on a street that is restricted during such emergencies. Expect a huge fine and probably a towing bill.

The transitory life takes a toll on many levels. Our country has a long history of hating those we send to represent us. Unless your representative is wealthy, he or she is managing to live in two places simultaneously, living a very public life, and trying to do the job. As citizens, we often think they're off living the high life. But I can assure you, they are not.

THIS PLACE AIN'T
ON THE LEVEL

As NEW MEMBERS COME to Congress, you see their eyes filled with idealism. They analyze the problems and set off at full speed to find a way to fix them. They are often frustrated by the way the Congress operates and they often remind me of a story told to me about Jimmy Burke, Massachusetts politician. It the 1980s, Jimmy Burke represented the 13th Congressional district in Boston. Another member of the Massachusetts delegation was the first openly gay member of the United States House of Representatives, named Gerry Studds. Jimmy Burke was old-style Boston politician who smoked a cigar and was not very elegant in his appearance. He watched Gerry Studds very carefully for a long time. One day he called Studds over to him and said, "Gerry, come here. I want to tell you something."

Studds came over and sat down and said, "What do you want to tell me?

Burke looked at him for a long time and then said, "Gary you are a new congressman. You're smart. You work hard, and you have good ideas, but there's something you're missing."

Studds said, "What's that?"

Jimmy Burke said, "Jerry, this place ain't on the level. Don't ever forget that."

This story carries lots of wisdom for new members. If they are going to succeed, they must learn the rules and ask questions of people they don't trust. Moving forward without asking questions can lead to bad results. Voters want their representatives to make a difference immediately, but it doesn't happen that way.

In 2002, I was planning a trip to Iraq to assess what I thought the outcome of our invasion might be. I asked the Speaker, Tom Foley (D-WA), if he had any advice. He, said, without hesitation, "Don't go!"

I said, "Mr. Speaker, I'm committed to go, so do you have any advice." He pondered a moment and then said, "Let me tell you a story about Ambassador Joe Wilson in a meeting he had with Saddam Hussein. When you meet the Iraqi leader, the Iraqis will instruct you to stand in a certain place with your toes on a line. When Saddam meets you, you must bend forward, keeping your toes on the line as you shake hands. Ambassador Wilson realized the optics of such an act. He would appear in photos as if he was bowing to Saddam, thus acknowledging his superiority. Joe Wilson shifted his feet so they were parallel to the line and did not bend to shake Saddam's hand." He extended his hand laterally and shook Saddam's hand. The picture did not satisfy Saddam."

Had I met Saddam on that trip and not had that advice, the title on the picture of our meeting would have read, *Congressman Bows to Saddam*.

The trip had another outcome. Some months before, in a large press conference on the steps of the Longworth building, I said that George W. Bush was so eager to go to war in Iraq that he would lie about weapons of mass destruction. This statement was never reported in Washington, D.C., or Seattle. But be aware that a representative's comments are never forgotten if they are captured on tape or digitized. You probably see what's coming.

Months later, while visiting Iraq, I got a call from George Stephanopoulos from ABC News, asking for an interview. I knew him from his days in the House as a legislative aid to Dick Gebhardt, so I said yes. On that day, I was standing in ninety-degree sunshine on the roof of the Iraqi government communications building. His first question to me was this: "Jim, do really believe that the President will tell a lie to the American people to go to war?"

I remembered what I had said several months before, so I knew George had me in a bind. If I said no, he would play my previous statement, making me look foolish. If I said yes, he would put me in the position of calling the President a liar while on Iraqi soil.

I told George, "I think the President will mislead the American people into war."

If I had listened to Tom and not gone to Iraq, I could have saved myself some grief. Tom knew that Iraq was not on the level, and he tried to tell me. I just didn't hear it. So I became Baghdad Jim, somewhat reminiscent of Hanoi Jane Fonda.

In politics, this is another case where I am reminded of that old aphorism in medicine from the father of American medicine, William Osler: "Listen to the patient. He is telling you what is the matter with him."

Politicians can learn a lot if they keep their mouth shut and listen.

If You Want to be a Star, Forget Bipartisanship

THERE ARE TWO KINDS of politicians: those who want to be stars and those who want to accomplish something. You can quickly spot the former. Politicians who want to be stars are visible because they are not interested in bipartisanship. During the time I was in the Washington State Legislature, from 1970 to 1987, and then in the Congress, from 1989 to 1994, there was great bipartisanship in many legislative bodies across the country. When Newt Gingrich came to the Congress in 1984, he assessed the political situation and came to the conclusion that bipartisanship would never lead to a Republican takeover of Congress. He decided that for the Republicans to take over, there had to be an end to bipartisanship.

In the early 1980s, Gingrich began his assault on bipartisanship by attacking members of the Democratic caucus through charges of ethics violations. A long series of attacks were made in the late 1980s. Accusations were leveled at Democratic members on issues including financial corruption, sexual activities, and other violations of House rules. The ethics committee was central to this attack on the Democratic caucus. The goal was clear; he wanted to disgrace the Democratic caucus.

When I arrived in Congress there were charges circulating against Dan Rostenkowski (D-IL), Charlie Wilson (D-TX), Tom Foley, and members who had accounts in the House bank. The House bank was established sometime in the 1850s to deal with the problems of members who were living in Washington, D.C., far from their home banking establishment. Members' paychecks were deposited in the bank, and members wrote checks to cover their various financial obligations.

Not infrequently, a member's account would be overdrawn, sometimes because a spouse had written a check. Or, members knew paychecks were coming in a day or two, and they wrote checks assuming that the account would receive the money before the check would reach its destination. This process functioned as a rudimentary overdraft protection, which was a service offered by most banks at that time. Members were routinely called by the Sergeant at Arms staff to inform them that their account was overdrawn. Deposits were made, and no money was ever lost.

This situation was characterized by Newt Gingrich as a corrupt bank that the Democratic Party was running in the House of Representatives. The Ethic Committee initiated an investigation, and I was one of four members who looked over all 435 accounts. The banking scandal, as it was called, was so toxic that all members records were opened up for public view. The perception of members bouncing checks was perceived by the public as a horrible perk that members of Congress enjoyed. The result was dozens of members lost their seats in the next Congress. Newt Gingrich didn't care how many Republicans lost because he knew that more Democrats would lose, and therefore, the scandal would increase his chances to take over the House. This all occurred in the session of 1991–1992.

In this session of 1993–1994, Bill Clinton was the new president. Charges were brought against Dan Rostenkowski, and once again the Ethics Committee was charged with the investigation of his alleged corruption. I was the chairman of the Ethics Committee during that period, having been appointed by Speaker Foley.

During this same period, the Congress was considering a universal health care program presented by Mrs. Clinton. The Republicans were desperate to kill this plan because they believed that if the Congress passed health care for all, the public would support them without question, and the Republicans would never have a chance to take over power in the House. The history of success of the Democratic Party since the passage of the Social Security act of 1935 was an ominous sign to the Republicans that if the Democrats succeeded, they would face another sixty years with the Democrats in power. That is why Trump and the Republicans are so dead set against Obamacare today.

The Democrats struggled during the session of 1993–1994, just as they did in 2009–2010, to enact health care for all. The bill was poised to pass out of the Ways and Means Committee, of which Dan Rostenkowski was the chairman. Dan Rostenkowski was arguably the most powerful man in the House. We may never know why the Justice Department decided to bring charges in federal court against Dan Rostenkowski at that moment. This threw the Congress into a massive state of confusion, and no vote was ever taken on the floor of the House on health care for all. Mrs. Clinton's effort failed here. Remember, it is always easier to kill legislation than it is to sign it into law.

In order to deal with the economic problems of the country, President Clinton proposed new taxes, which were needed to reduce the national debt. The tax bill was passed without a single Republican vote, and it set us on a course over the next six years to have our first budget surplus in many years. However, the campaign of 1994 was a referendum on the corrupt Democratic House caucus. Newt Gingrich succeeded in that election, and the Republicans took over for the first time in forty years.

Every freshman class in the past had an orientation at the Kennedy school of Government, where issues were presented from the right, center, and the left. The Kennedy School faculty was careful not to present a biased approach to any issue, whether it was the environment, taxes, energy, war, or whatever. To strengthen his partisan approach to government, in January 1995, Newt Gingrich took the Republican freshmen to the American Heritage Institute to keep them ideologically pure.

Prior to 1995, bills and appropriations were done on a bipartisan basis on most occasions. After the election of 1994, the Republicans, and particularly the Speaker, controlled the flow of legislation that largely excluded participation by committees and especially by Democratic members. The Democrats quickly learned what the nature of the new Congress was to be: partisan in everything.

Suddenly the air was filled with numerous ethical complaints against Newt Gingrich. Since that time, the Congress has been in almost continuous combat in the Ethics Committee. Members on both sides of the aisle have been attacked for matters large and small, with the only real goal being to smear the other side.

If you think about power as one of the elements that drives members' participation in the political process, it is easy to see that partisanship is the best way to get power. Bipartisanship, by its very nature, suggests power sharing, and Newt realized that a minority can never get control in a bipartisan arrangement. There will always be more left and center leaning Democrats than there are right leaning Republicans.

One example from the Appropriations Committee illustrates this concept. The subcommittee chairmen of the Appropriations Committee are called "Cardinals." The Cardinals would sit down with their ranking member, who is the highest seniority member of the minority party, and allocations would be made of the money to be appropriated in that area. The majority member would control seventy percent of the money, and the minority member would control thirty percent of the money. This bipartisan approach gave the minority some impact on the process, and more importantly, it did not exclude them totally.

When Newt took over, these allocations were no longer made. Funding decisions were made totally by the Speaker and his leadership group. This style of leadership persisted to the speakership of Dennis Hastert (R-IL). It was largely implemented by his majority leader, Tom DeLay (R-TX), who took over the day-to-day running of the House.

During the period from 1995 until 2007, the House of Representatives was run on a strictly partisan basis. The Republican members were disciplined if they voted with the Democrats, so the moderate Republicans found it increasingly difficult to remain in the House and vote as they saw fit to represent their constituents. The Republican caucus took on the appearance of the parliamentary systems like Great Britain or other European countries.

After twelve years of this regime, Democrats won control in 2006. Most of the new members coming in, or those that had been elected in the previous twelve years, knew no other form of legislative operation. The process established by Newt Gingrich has been continued by the Democratic leadership. Older members who remembered a previous style of operation tried to reestablish the old system in some instances, but it was always overridden by decisions made at the leadership level. The regular order of legislation, which exists in the rules, was largely abandoned, first by Gingrich, and then by the subsequent Democratic leadership. Absolute power was the goal of both sides. Members who were elected and wanted absolute power were pleased. Members, who understood that a democracy cannot solve the complicated problems it faces by looking to only one side of the issue were, and are, very frustrated.

Barak Obama tried to reestablish the principal of bipartisanship. His hope was that this nation could solve its problems by having all sides heard in the debate. The first session showed the Republicans refusal to relinquish the strategy of partisanship as they said, "No! No! No."

I am at a loss to suggest how this grab for absolute power can be changed. I sometimes believe that only a real catastrophe for this country will cause us to seek the common good. To do that, we must listen to everyone as we make decisions in our government. The majority will ultimately make the decisions, but the process of listening to disagreeing views is important, particularly if we are to find answers that work and are acceptable to the population.

A VENDETTA IN THE
CONGRESS, 1993–2007

YESTERDAY AT MY NEIGHBORHOOD coffee shop a friend handed me a gift. It was John Boehner's memoir, *On the House: A Washington Memoir*. Like every politician who picks up a political book, I turned to the index, and I was stunned to find that my name wasn't listed.

I know history is written by the winners, so a memoir has the pleasure of leaving things out that don't fit the narrative. However, if anyone cares for a more "complete history," it struck me that it might be useful to tell the story of my twelve-year court battle with John Boehner from my perspective. I suspect it looks very different to him. But maybe he and I can talk about it over a glass of *vin rouge* someday.

It all began when I came to Congress in 1988, and Tom Foley, my friend since 1970, was Speaker. I came to Congress to work on single payer health care, similar to many European systems that covered all citizens. I knew that several committees had some health care jurisdiction, and I chose as my goal a seat on the Ways and Means Committee. They had the Medicare portfolio and part of the Medicaid portfolio, so I told Tom I wanted to be on Ways and Means.

He told me no for two reasons: First, Danny Rostenkowski would not allow a freshman on the committee. He wanted to watch me for one term to find out if I would be a team player. Chairmen don't appreciate new members who "know it all" and won't listen to guidance. The second reason, Tom told me, was that Ben Cardin (D-MD) from Baltimore was already in line ahead of me. Ben was a former Speaker of the House in the Maryland Assembly and was patiently waiting for his chance. When Dick Gephardt (D-MO) left the committee to become the Majority Leader, I asked again. Same answer. Ben Cardin got the seat on the committee.

I got re-elected in 1990, and Tom appointed me to the Ways and Means Committee. Less than a month later Tom called me to ask if I would accept an appointment to the Ethics Committee. The first rule in politics is when someone looks out for you, then you have a debt to pay. It is not an evil *quid pro quo*. It is just good human behavior to remember who helped you.

I did not want to sit in judgement over my colleagues, but I did not have the option to say "no." During the next two years, I sat through the agonies of the investigation of the House bank debacle on a subcommittee with Ben Cardin. We disagreed on how many of our colleagues we should throw under the bus. The other members watched us and decided that Ben was not protective enough of members.

In the 1993–1994 House session, the distinguished chair of the Ethics Committee, who was a retired judge from Cleveland, named Lou Stokes (D-OH), begged Tom to let him off the committee. Ben Cardin was senior and was about to be appointed chair of the committee. The other members of the committee quietly rebelled. They went to Tom Foley and told him they would resign if Ben became the chairman.

So in 1993, Tom Foley appointed me co-chair of the Ethics Committee after only four years of service in the Congress. At the end of the 1993–1994 session, Newt Gingrich asked for Ethics Committee approval of a proposal to use 501(c)(3) money to launch a teaching and television educational TV course accompanied by distribution of teaching materials to a wide range of outlets.

I was concerned, along with the co-chair, Fred Grandy (R-IA), about the mixing of tax-deductible 501(c)(3) money with any project that would be used for primarily political organizing, which would be a violation of Federal Law and House rules and regulation. A strong letter was written to the Speaker, cautioning against any project that did not follow all applicable laws, Federal regulations, and rules of the House. We granted approval based on these caveats. Newt Gingrich proceeded with his project at Georgia State University.

As a result of the election of 1994, the Republicans took control of the House of Representatives. Nancy Johnson (R-CT) was appointed co-chair of the Ethics committee to serve along with me. In January 1995, Newt Gingrich was flying high. Newt was approached by Rupert Murdoch with a controversial multimillion dollar book deal, which the committee made him turn down. During the next two years, the committee was flooded with ethics complaints filed by outside groups as well as Democratic members of the House. As the co-chair of a five Republican, five Democrat committee, I had the job of creating a fair and balanced process to deal with Newt's alleged transgressions.

We dismissed numerous complaints, but one issue could not be dismissed, and finally a special Counsel, James Cole, was appointed, on a bipartisan basis, to the investigative subcommittee. Cole's charge was to review the charges related to the college course in which it was alleged that Newt Gingrich had commingled both tax deductible and taxable moneys, thus breaking the tax laws of the United States. This was done after receiving the 1993 letter from Fred Grandy and me.

Despite repeated Republican efforts to clear the Speaker of all charges without adequate investigation, I forced Nancy Johnson, co-chair, to proceed with the investigation in a thorough fashion. The rules required the appointment of an investigative subcommittee. Porter Goss (R-FL), Steve Schiff (R-NM), Ben Cardin (D-MD), and Nancy Pelosi (D-CA) were appointed. This committee operated in secrecy for nearly a year and found merit in various charges. The penalty was a fine of $300,000. In addition, part of the investigation's resolution was an agreement that the Speaker would not orchestrate a response in the press to minimize the punishment meted out by the committee.

Before this resolution was discussed in the full committee so that all members would know the results, the Speaker organized a conference call in mid-December with the Republican leadership, including John Boehner and other lawyers and staff personnel. This was done within twenty-four hours of signing an agreement that he would not do so. John Boehner, on a trip to Florida, stopped at a restaurant, sent his family in to eat, and sat in the car, using his analog phone to participate in this conference call. This fateful December day's phone call was taped by two local residents, John and Alice Martin. Parenthetically, it seems that the Martins were sitting in their truck, trying to catch any phone calls from their allegedly philandering son-in-law.

The taped conference call seemed like an important call, but they did not know who to give it to. This tape was a hot potato that bounced around Washington, D.C., in several offices, including that of the Minority Leader, David Bonior (D-MI). Finally, it arrived in the office of their actual Congresswoman, Karen Thurman (D-FL). She told the Martins to give it to me. The Martins had come to Washington, D.C., to witness the swearing in of a Congressman, Allan Boyd (D-FL), whom they had help elect. They were grassroots activists who were union members in Florida.

The beginning of the 1997 session was very tense and tumultuous. The Speaker of the House was under investigation by the Ethics Committee, and he wanted the matter before the Ethics Committee resolved before the Congress was sworn in. The first thing that happens in every new Congress is the election of the Speaker, and the Speaker's concern was that members on his side would be unwilling to vote for him while there was an ethics cloud hanging over his head. He needed to resolve this issue before he could ask the members to vote for him.

The full Ethics Committee met on January 10, to receive the report of the investigative subcommittee. I had been in Italy for the month of December, and I did not know what the Committee had decided. The House rules precluded the subcommittee from reporting their decision, except in full session. The procedure was designed to be like a grand jury.

The meeting was long and contentious, and when the committee took a break, the Martins appeared in the hallway outside of the Ethics Committee and asked if I was there. Before I was introduced to them, they handed me an envelope and said, "Here is a tape that we would like you to listen to." I asked who they were, and they identified themselves, saying they had come to the swearing in of congressman, Alan Boyd. I thanked them, and they walked away. I had never seen them before or since. They apparently identified themselves to the press and to the Justice Department as the people responsible for the illegal taping of a private conversation. They were fined $500 each.

I took the tape to my office, listened to it, and I was stunned to hear the Speaker not only orchestrating the response in violation of the agreement but discussing it with individuals from outside the Congress before a report had been given to the full Committee. I agreed with the Martins' assessment of the importance of the tape. I thought the people had a right to know about the Speaker's actions, and I called reporters from national daily newspapers. I made no press release or accusations. I simply gave two reporters a chance to hear the tape. The *New York Times* reporter taped the recording as it was being played. The *Atlantic Constitution* reporter took copious notes. No tapes were made or given out.

Newt was very worried about the effect of the $300,000 fine by the Ethics Committee on his re-election as Speaker. The Republicans had lost a number of seats in the 1996 election, and Newt was insecure. At this time, he decided to reorder his leadership team and dumped John Boehner in favor of J.C. Watts (R-OK), who was the only black representative in the Republican caucus. Gingrich wanted diversity and John Boehner was expendable.

At this time, no one knew that John Boehner was on the call. He never spoke. Then, he revealed that he was in Florida on an unsecured phone, and that he was the source of the leaked attempt by Gingrich to get his leadership to soften the impact of a $300,000 fine on his upcoming election.

The Justice Department investigated accusations arising from my role in releasing the tape, but no charges were filed, and the case was dropped. Not satisfied with this result, the House leadership, including Gingrich, encouraged John Boehner to file a civil lawsuit, despite the fact that he had been demoted from a leadership post in the Republican caucus. Perhaps because of his demotion and humiliation, Boehner accepted this challenge, believing that he could rehabilitate himself in the eyes of leadership by going after me.

Boehner was never identified in the press accounts. We will never know how Boehner came to publicly confess that he was the fool who listened in on an unsecured phone, but he took full blame. Thus, he was anointed as the one to pursue justice.

The Republicans framed it quickly as an invasion of privacy, even though it was common knowledge that cell phones were unsecured. Around this time, there was a much publicized similar incident in which the Prince of Wales was recorded talking to his mistress while he was still married to Princess Diana.

I knew that members of Congress were protected by a speech and debate clause of the Constitution for what they do on the floor and in committee. John Boehner also knew that the Supreme Court had defined Freedom of Speech rules in the *New York Times* case. If material is given out, (1) it must be true, (2) it must be of public importance, and (3) the giver of the information must have done nothing illegal to obtain the information.

On all counts, I was in the clear. I had been handed the tape in the hallway of the Capitol by people I did not know. But more importantly, I had given it to the *New York Times,* who had judged it to be true and of public importance.

So why would John Boehner pursue such a lawsuit? In later negotiations with me, Boehner revealed that Porter Goss and David Hobson (R-OH), members of the Ethics Committee, encouraged him in his suit, and really, they were the ones standing in the way of settlement. They insisted that I should admit that I had no First Amendment Right of Free Speech. They demanded an admission of guilt while a trial on damages was wending its way through the Federal courts. It appeared that Boehner was always their pawn, whom they used even after Gingrich was dumped as Speaker.

My lawyers said, "Don't talk because what you say will make it harder to defend you." Politically, what Gingrich wanted was an admission of guilt so that he could institute a motion on the floor to have me expelled from the House for having broken the law.

The suit that John Boehner brought was a historic first for the House. For the first time, the Ethics committee gave Boehner permission to sue personally another member of Congress, using campaign funds. So, dueling in the courts became the new order of the day in Congress.

When the case was filed, I moved for immediate dismissal under the First Amendment and Judge Thomas Hogan granted this motion. More on Judge Hogan later.

The Republican leadership was not satisfied with this result, and it was appealed to the D.C. Circuit Court of Appeals. The three judges were Judge David Sentelle (who chaired the committee that removed the first Special Prosecutor for President Clinton and engineered the selection of Ken Starr), Judge Ginsburg, and Judge Randolph. This court by a 2–1 vote denied the First Amendment protection. More interesting than the result was the fact that Judge Sentelle supported the First Amendment defense, but the other two Judges, although rejecting the First

Amendment defense, could themselves not agree on the reasons for their objection.

On at least three separate occasions before and after the Supreme Court decision, I sent emissaries (Congressmen Miller and Rangel) to Boehner to try to settle the case. At one point, Boehner and I met at least five times to work out a solution. I wrote several different apologies to be read on the floor. Boehner would never put anything in writing, but his response was always the same: "Porter Goss won't accept this. You must admit you did wrong and give me $10,000 for charity."

This is the offer he bragged about, which he knew was unacceptable. It would have left me open to censure by the House and possible criminal action. They were in court determining whether I had First Amendment rights of free speech, and he already had one decision in his favor.

Boehner never made an offer that had any chance of acceptance, and he knew it. To prove his disingenuousness, he began talking to the press about their secret discussions. For a guy who was worried about his privacy, he certainly acted strangely by giving the story to the press. There was never a sincere effort on his part to settle this case.

The case was immediately appealed from the Appeals Court to the US Supreme Court, where it was accepted, although a similar case, *Volper v. Bartnicki*, was taken for adjudication. The Supreme Court by a 6–3 decision ruled in favor of the First Amendment and referred *Boehner v. McDermott* back to the Circuit Court for review under the precedent set by the *Volper* decision. To see the true reasons for pursuing this case, one need look no further than the request by the three same D.C. Circuit Court judges who had just been reversed by the Supreme Court to have the case referred back to them.

This panel proceeded to ignore the Supreme Court, allowing a totally new line of attack: that congressmen had a higher duty than an ordinary citizen, and therefore was not protected by the Constitution. They referred it back to the trial court of Judge Hogan.

I am not a lawyer, and I was unaware of the Federalist Society, a group of right-wing judges and conservative lawyers who do most of the planning for the conservative wing of the Republican party. However, I got my masters' degree in law and legal community politics in this trial process. Almost all recent appointments to the bench have been recommended to the Republican President by this society. More on this later.

After a period of fact finding by depositions, both sides filed for summary judgment: Boehner for damages and I filed for dismissal under the First Amendment protection.

This time Judge Hogan reversed himself and found that the First Amendment did not protect me. He awarded $10,000 statutory damages and $50,000 punitive damages. He held in abeyance the awarding of attorneys' fees until a pending appeal could be argued and decided. However, Boehner had entered an affidavit for $530,000 in attorneys' fees.

I appealed again to the Circuit Court of Appeals in D.C. Boehner entered a motion to get his favorite judges again. The legal fix was in, as they say in Chicago. Boehner won, so the case returned to the same three-judge panel, and by a vote of 2–1 (Sentelle dissenting) Judge Hogan's decision was affirmed.

This victory for Boehner meant that I had to pay the lawyer's fees for Boehner plus the fine. But the Sentelle dissent was so compelling that an *en banc* hearing (all nine judges) was sought.

While this case was going through the courts, another Ohio colleague of Boehner, David Hobson, filed an Ethics complaint against me. The Committee considered the case and found no violation of the rule, but they suggested there was a violation of the *spirit* of the rule. It was on the basis of a violation of the spirit of the rule that the court reached the decision that I had given up my First Amendment rights.

The significance of the ruling by the House Ethics Committee is this: The Constitution of the United States sets up the separation of powers, which is the basis for the operation of our government. Article 1 sets up Congress, giving Congress the right to write its own rules and enforce them. The Congress has always operated independently from the federal court system. The federal courts have always refused to interpret or to enforce the rules of the House or Senate.

The unique aspect of this case is that, for the first time in history, the Federal courts stepped in and interpreted a House rule thereby taking away my constitutional protections to the right of free speech. The court (5–4) found that I had First Amendment protection, but because I accepted voluntarily the secrecy limitation of the House rules by agreeing to serve on the Ethics Committee, I gave up my right of free speech. It was a historic decision.

Judge David Sentelle's dissent on this decision was again compelling, and an appeal was considered. After long discussions about the advisability of appealing the decision of the Circuit Court of Appeals, I decided not to appeal. The most compelling reason was that the right of free speech for the press had been protected. The question of whether the courts would overrule the decision by the Circuit Court to pierce a firewall between the legislative branch and the judicial branch was an open debate that could have led to a longer court case. Free speech protection for the press was at risk.

The result of a twelve-year lawsuit was that the standards for the exercise of free speech were protected for the press, but the congressman who brought the case was a casualty of a novel interpretation of the power of the Federal courts. This interpretation will be tested at some later date, but to prolong this case at this point would simply expose me to further costs. I paid $60,000 in damages and more than $1.1 million in attorney's fees to John Boehner. It was a small price to pay to protect the right of free speech for all Americans.

This was not a meaningless squabble between two Congressmen. It ws a Machiavellian attempt to silence dissent. Boehner never alleged any damages whatsoever. Gingrich and Hobson's intention clearly was to restrict the First Amendment. Attack anyone who dares to reveal a Republican leader's lack of integrity. Gingrich was violating his agreement even before most of the Ethics Committee knew about the agreement. His promissory word was proven worthless.

Fate gave me the role of initiating the ethics process, which led to a $300,000 fine for Newt. Two years later, Newt was gone from elective office, a victim of his own hubris. Some may question the purely political formulation of the case, but if you accept the fact that Boehner never mentioned damages once in ten years, and he refused to give any alternative proposal to resolve the case, and that his Ohio sidekick, David Hobson, filed a separate ethics complaint, you begin to see the pattern. As an aside, the ethics complaint was resolved in December 2007 by a statement that ethical violation occurred, and no further action would be taken. They made the distinction that only the spirit of the law had been broken. So much for the House Rules.

You might ask how there was a violation, but no punishment was exacted. Perhaps serendipitously, Speaker Hastert, who followed Newt was caught in a sex scandal and an ethics charge had been brought. He wanted out of Congress as quickly as possible, and the exchange for his dismissal was done at the same time I got my "broke the spirit of the Rules" dismissal by the committee.

The use of House rules in a civil litigation opens up a whole new realm for the courts to erode the separation of powers. Every member of any committee that requires secrecy is now open to criminal or civil litigation. Representatives who attend top secret briefings give up their First Amendment protections. Think about it.

CSI: SPECIAL UNIT ON ABUSE OF POWER

WITH AMERICA'S ATTENTION DIVERTED to the quagmire in Iraq, the Republican majority in Congress quietly instituted a new form of government in the United States called *Repocracy*, which I define as Republican party authoritarianism. Under *Repocracy*, Republicans try to stifle debate, stiff-arm democracy, and silence the American people.

For those of you who love to watch Congress and often wonder why things happen in a certain way, as in sports, the first rule is never taken your eye off the ball. Keep watching the floor of the House on C-Span with low sound in the corner of your screen.

Majority Leader Boehner put his stamp on the new *Repocracy* in the House. Longtime House courtesy requires that the Majority Leader discuss with the Minority Leader any changes contemplated in action on the floor.

John Boehner, without notice, announced that he was going to change the operation of the House with respect to the length of votes. For as long as anyone on the floor can remember, the voting machines have been open for fifteen minutes so that people can come from their offices to vote. Often these "fifteens" are followed by five-minute votes in order to speed the process up. The votes are usually stacked so as not to take too much of the members' time.

On March 16, 2006, things were not moving fast enough in the House to please the Leader from K Street. There was a big fundraiser that night, so Boehner put the pedal to the metal to get the House moving. He asked for unanimous consent to reduce the voting time to two minutes. He made his request on the floor when no one expected it, so no one was quick enough to object. Really, it was a slick grab of power. With 435 members in a small room, two minutes is not even enough time to walk across the room to question someone about their thinking before the vote is over.

But then, why would someone want to talk to another member in the Congress anyway? Vote your prejudice, or ignorance, or how the leadership tells you to vote and then off to the fundraising. God forbid, there might be some debate in the Congress. Democracy is being exchanged for *Repocracy*. The government of the *Repocracy* meets less and less; and when it does meet, it is only to rubberstamp the President's insidious policies. Consider the fact that the voting machine was left open for many hours while the leadership broke arms, as in the Medicare vote of several years ago. But if we are in such a hurry to gather in fundraising gold for the campaign, the voting time must be limited to two minutes.

The word, Congress, comes from the Latin *con+egresso,* which means come together. The idea was that there would be orderly and reasoned debate. You be the judge whether or not we have a functioning Congress today. Perhaps we could stay an extra day each week and discuss health care, surveillance, torture, global warming, and a few other issues like the 500,000 new children who are living in poverty in this *Repocracy*.

While some Americans haven't been looking, our democracy has been replaced by a weak lapdog that is reminiscent of the Parliaments of Germany and Italy in the 1920s and 1930s. They were democratically elected, but they gave up their policy and oversight roles as they, like lapdogs, rolled over for the leaders of impenetrable juntas of business and the unitary executive.

These paragraphs summarize my observations in Congress from several years ago, but they accurately describe the Congress today. The erosion of democracy has continued at a rapid pace as we have watched the efficacy of the Congress fade. Budgets don't get passed. Everything is done by continuing resolution. This is a clever maneuver to hide the cutting of government while holding the spending at last year's level. If a program, like the military budget is favored, it can be increased in other ways. Cutting the military means you are not supportive of a strong defense. No intelligent member would want to be accused of that in a campaign advertisement.

Climate concerns never get addressed because that takes time and thought and might rile up contributors. The same could be said of other environmental concerns, or opioid addiction, or voter suppression, or poor school performance, or universal health care. None of these issues are addressed, and the people get angry and turn to a strong man who promises to "drain the swamp in Washington" and make "America Great Again."

There is no mystery where Trump came from. He is a political reaction to a failed Congress dominated by Senate rules that were put in place to allow an increasingly diminishing white minority to maintain control over political power. Voting rules are controlled by states, and the filibuster is used in the Senate to prevent federal legislation to protect the right to vote.

The advent of the internet with social media monopolies has only accelerated the destruction of democracy. We shall see if the Senate repeals its restrictive rules and passes laws to repair voting rights nationwide. Will we ever have a hearing on the question of removing the electoral college? Maybe if Texas turns blue, but don't hold your breath.

MYTHS AND POWER

MYTHS ARE THE ESSENCE of history. Politics is based on myths. Politicians spend their time creating myths to explain the world and themselves. The enlightenment was a nodal point in history. At that point in time, humans began to use the scientific method, which made it possible to separate myths based on belief and facts based on scientific observation. Experiments are often an attempt to prove or disprove a belief that is strongly held.

Historians spend endless hours trying to untangle myth from actual facts and events. History is always written by the winners, so it is never clear if there is any objective truth. It depends on your viewpoint.

In every society there are fearful and distrustful leaders. It is often found in people who have not been trustworthy in the past. Because they know how they have secretly behaved, they expected the same in others. Corrupt leaders have little ability to hold the trust of the people so they must find an enemy on which to focus the people's attention.

At times the problems of the selection process are so acute that a diversionary action must be created to divert the people's attention. There must always be a cause or event to justify extreme political action.

The slogans that justify war are burned into our memories to carry out their manifest destiny given to them by God, like, *Remember the Maine*, *Pearl Harbor*, *The Gulf of Tonkin* and the *WMDs of Saddam Hussein*. Often on the front page of the *New York Times*, we see, once again, a lie being fed to people in order that one of the God-blessed nations may invade or attack. Groups that are rabid don't see others as fully human and so can do anything to each other. Slavery, apartheid separation, deprivation of land and birthright are a consequence.

I am Irish, and I understand the myths between the religions of Britain and Ireland. For 600 years there was endless pain and killing as one religion tried to crush another in God's name. Irish Alzheimer's is defined as, "*we forgot everything but the grudge*." But on April 10, 1998 the Good Friday Accords were signed to end the endless killing. It is not perfect, and Brexit has scraped the scab off a bit, but so far so good.

I served in Congress for twenty-eight years and heard politicians try to weave the myth of a two-state solution in the Middle East. After watching carefully and travelling all over the region in person, I'm convinced neither side was willing to actually agree to a fair resolution of this ancient myth.

The myth that the North American continent was empty of civilization, which gave the US the right to ethnically cleanse the land to the Pacific and to disregard claims of Spaniards who had claimed land in the southwest in previous years. British slaughter of aboriginal people in Australia was enabled by the myth of *Terra Nullius*. It meant that there were no human beings in the land, so hunting aboriginals was accepted under British law. This was ended only by a 1967 Australian referendum.

I can remember having a conversation about the Middle East situation in 1992. I suggested to two colleagues that war would continue until we have honest negotiations without preconditions.

As an ordinary citizen looking into Congress, this great hall of myths, it is extremely important to figure out your representative's mythology. One day in frustration, I said, "Whenever you begin to talk about the Middle East, ask the question, 'when does the history of Middle

East events start for you?' Is the answer 6000 B.C., or 1918, or 1934, or after World War II?" Each date includes or leaves out huge swaths of history, building its own myth.

In the Congress of 2021, the great lie of a stolen election has become the dominant myth for the Republican party. The myth of "voter fraud" and the need for more restrictive voting regulations at the state level has permeated conservative thinking right up to the Supreme Court, as articulated in Justice Samuel Alito's majority opinion in *Brnovich v. DNC*. The consequence of the myth is a weakening of the Voting Rights Act. Political myths have very real consequences. If you look beyond the myths, you'll see the real reason for mythmaking: Power.

A REMEDY: A MORE
HUMAN CONGRESS

IN CONGRESS, AS IN life, the past is more than
prologue. Even if Democrats sweep their races
this fall and send the balloons soaring, bitterness
and failure in Congress will not disappear. It
could, in fact, get worse.

Sam Rayburn famously said that any jackass
can kick a barn down, but it takes a carpenter
to put one up. Rayburn, a Texan, was Speaker
of the House three times between 1947 and
1961, and so he knew a good bit about barn
kicking. He held public office through two
world wars, the Great Depression, the Korean
War, the worst of the Cold War, early Vietnam,
and the fight for civil rights. He was Speaker of
the whole House, not just one party, and in his
time, Congress struggled but did great things.
He worked with southern conservatives and
liberal Republicans (an extinct species) not just
to "get things done" but to save the country in

real terms, again and again. The stakes are just as high today.

Those of us who were House members in the early 1990s know when Congress turned its back on such capability. It was not gradual. My own history, spanning 1988 to 2017, witnessed the entire era of decline, down to the election of Trump and his embrace by the GOP. This is an era that absolutely must be understood.

Twenty-seven years ago, when the most world-changing event of the late twentieth century took place—when the Soviet Union, America's existential enemy, collapsed and the Cold War came to an end—the US Congress barely reacted. No dancing and sharing of cake beneath chandeliers. There were hardly a few collaborative efforts to help welcome and shape a new global landscape. Instead, Congress went to war against itself, and won.

Between 1992 and year 1994, when Republicans won the House for the first time in forty years, a group of far-right conservatives under Newt Gingrich embroiled Congress and the nation in a series of trumped up scandals that deeply damaged the image of the institution, both in the eyes of the public and its own members. In the following years, while war and genocide in the Balkans and Rwanda, economic collapse in Russia, the first US budget surplus in three decades, nuclear tests by Pakistan and India, and terrorist threats from Islamic radicals abroad and far right extremists at home, in Oklahoma City, all emerged, a GOP-led Congress was obsessed with obstructing and demonizing a popular Democratic president, Bill Clinton. And in 1999, it dragged the nation through a humiliating, despicable impeachment in front of the whole world, while Speaker Gingrich was himself forced out of Congress for ethics violations.

Gingrich showed Republicans how to win, and to keep winning, and they learned the lesson. When commentators today say that Donald Trump doesn't care about the liberal world order, they might recall that this has been true of GOP conservatives for some time. Those who might argue that foreign policy is the province of the Executive forget that Congress has many committees—Armed Services, Foreign Affairs, Intelligence, Energy and Commerce, Science and Space—with deep concern in global matters.

It has also been said that Gingrich and his followers "broke Congress." This isn't quite right. What they did was destroy a culture of working relations—the "barn" that had been built by both parties to see America through a war-torn century. It was clear to many of us in the 1990s that Gingrich, Dick Armey (R-TX), and their band of angry men, didn't worry about any of that. Nor were they interested in limited government, like Ronald Reagan (who, though venerated by the right ever after, was able to work consistently with Democratic Speaker Tip O'Neill). But if they demolished what Democrats had built and changed the norms of inter-party behavior, they could demolish the builders and rule in their place. This was made clear to me in an early speech Gingrich gave to College Republicans, where he said: "Every one of you is old enough to have been a rifleman in Vietnam...This is the same business. We're just lucky, in this country, we don't use bullets, we use ballots instead. You're fighting a war. It is a war for power."

I was in politics for twenty years before I came to the Capitol, and though state legislatures aren't known for refined exchanges of opinion, we never spoke in such terms. Politics was messy, toilsome, exasperating, but above all transactional: to get something you wanted, you had to give up something else; and to give up something meant you were owed. Treating the other party like an existential enemy meant burning down the barn. It also meant denigrating the people who had voted for those representatives.

Those words by Gingrich reveal one side of what has happened in Congress. Yes, the 1990s were also when the South rose again, when its conservatives joined the GOP in bulk. But the war has not stopped; no quarter has been given. Democrats never fully understood this. We were used to water balloons, sometimes mud, thrown around, and then, this group shows up with automatic weapons and begins shooting. We weren't ready—and still aren't, mainly because of what it means—to fight like this, conceiving ever new ways to bend and break the rules of our democracy, even on something so fundamental as voting rights, to sacrifice everything, including the public good, for power.

The other side of the war relates to ideas, those driving why the conflict must be fought to the death. The most concise statement I know about this was made in a speech by Dick Armey, when he became House Majority Leader in 1995: "Behind our New Deals and New Frontiers and Great Societies you find, with a difference only in power and nerve, the same sort of person who gave the world its Five-Year Plans and Great Leaps Forward." Here are FDR, JFK, and LBJ revealed as Lenin, Stalin, and Mao.

What does it take to think this way? Equating US presidents with some of the greatest monsters in history? We foolishly took it as rhetoric at the time. But Armey meant what he said, and so have many Republicans who came after, down to the Tea Party and later. Gingrich, the strategist, never believed such poison, calling those of such mind who voted him out "jihadists" and "cannibals." He didn't seem to understand what he'd unleashed. Armey's words were the revelation that true extremism was already darkening the mainstream. Part of this extremism, already circulating in far right talk radio and the internet, was that liberals and moderates are terrible human beings, bent on destroying America, so any strategy is justified if it weakens their program and presence in government.

After he became Speaker in 1994, Gingrich immediately began to dismantle the House culture. These changes are worth remembering. The work week was cut to three-and-a-half days, sending members home Friday through Monday to mingle with constituents. This was paired with the canceling of all overseas trips. The real intent, and the impact, was to keep Republican members from spending time after work, on weekends, or traveling with their Democratic colleagues. Families didn't live in Washington any longer and didn't get to know one another via shared activities and get-togethers, as had been the rule. Members didn't buy property in Washington; instead they started sleeping in their offices. In fact, offices were also switched around to keep the parties physically separated. Barriers to collegiality went up and stayed up.

Contempt was central to the Republican Revolution and the Contract with America. Salaries from 1994 on were held low or frozen for members and support personnel. There were massive cuts in staff; Permanent Committees like Arms Services and Foreign Relations lost half their people—again, at the very moment when the US faced a new era in world history. Non-partisan bodies were heavily targeted. They killed the Office of Technology Assessment, the only impartial source of expertise on scientific matters. This precedent has been followed by Donald Trump, who has no Science Advisor and has chopped by two-thirds the Office of Science and Technology Policy. Staff cuts continued through the 1990s, 2000s, into the 2010s, with the Congressional Budget Office and General Accountability Office losing nearly a third. Working for Congress has thus been treated as a substandard occupation (a reason for experienced aides to leave government for higher paid work at lobbying firms). Science, meanwhile, has been purposely exiled from any direct advisory role. So as the world has grown more complex and challenging, Congress has rigorously rendered itself more ignorant, incapable, biased, and parochial.

How do we change this? There are more than a few ideas out there, many of them quite good, about altering how we elect people, how to reduce the power of money, and more. I want to suggest something different. I entered Congress when things started to go wrong, when the barn began to splinter. What most struck me, as a psychiatrist, was how personal relationships among members of the two parties turned sour or vanished from importance.

Whatever else Congress might be, it is a place where human beings talk and interact. When that part of lawmaking breaks down, so does the institution. Change for the better requires that we improve this part of its culture. This means not only rules and procedures but for people to be brought together in non-hostile settings, including informal ones. It's easy to see a member you've never spoken to as an enemy, and conversely, it is extraordinarily difficult to do so if you know about their wife's or husband's recovery from a car accident, the story of their daughter's first job after college, or their old father failing with Alzheimer's, just like your mother-in-law.

One thing that Sam Rayburn did as Speaker was to continue a series of weekly after-hours meetings in the basement of the Capitol Building, room H-128. In this, he carried forward a tradition established under his predecessors, Republican Nicholas Longworth and Democrat John Garner. In the depths of the Great Depression, they employed the room as a type of elegant tavern (ignoring the eighteenth amendment ban on spirits), where members of both parties communed under the auspices of bourbon and branch water, telling stories, playing cards, making acquaintances, even talking politics, but all in an informal, off-the-record atmosphere.

The "Board of Education," as it was known, suggests the kind of cultural turn that Congress truly needs, on many levels. With so many members abandoning the institution, there should be little doubt about the need for a change in habitat. This won't happen suddenly, and it will take much courage. No single wave of Democrat victories, however progressive the victors, can dissolve away a generation of enmity. But it is certainly time to try and begin. Humanizing an institution that has forgotten how to be humane is a necessary part of a better Congress.

THE TOUGHEST VOTE

MEMORIAL DAY IS WHEN I remember that I gave President Bush the go ahead for the war on terror. On September 11, 2001, a group of Saudi religious fanatics commandeered four jetliners and launched attacks on the towers in New York, the Pentagon, and a site never to be known. Perhaps the White House or the Capitol Building itself was the goal. Nothing was done to confront our Saudi friends with the evil spawned in their country.

September 11, 2001, was a day of chaos in Washington and in the nation at large. The Constitution gives the power to declare war to the Congress. But over the years, this power has been given to the President by the inaction of the Congress. If you ask most Americans when we last declared war, if they have any idea, they say 1941 after Pearl Harbor. We did declare war against Japan, Germany, and Italy in December, 1941. But the last Congressional Declaration was in June, 1942, against Bulgaria, Hungary, and Romania.

But you say, "What about Korea, Vietnam, Grenada, or other places where troops have been sent?" A President can launch the country into war and then dare the Congress not to fund his actions. Ever since 1942, the President has been acting unilaterally.

A few days after the disastrous events in New York and Washington, D.C., George W. Bush came to the Congress and asked for a declaration of War on Terror. The Congress debated whether the President's proposal was too open ended, but in the end, many Democrats did vote for it. Many of us knew we were giving a blank check to an administration that was lusting for war. For those who were against it, we talked among ourselves about other approaches to the Saudi strike on America. Only one member of Congress, Barbara Lee from Oakland, California, voted "No." Voting "Yes" was the easy vote because if you voted "No," you would have to endlessly explain why you didn't support the President and the country in its moment of need. There is no vote I regret more than that vote.

This is the type of vote that reveals the true character of your representative. As we stood at the back of the chamber discussing how to vote, I will never forget the dean of the California delegation, Don Edwards, relating his anguish over voting for the Gulf of Tonkin resolution on August 7, 1964, which passed 416–0 in the House and 88–2 in the Senate. The only votes against it were by Ernest Gruening (D-AK) and Wayne Morse (D-OR). For Don, thirty-eight years of struggle were compressed into this day.

Senator Gruening objected at the time of the Gulf of Tonkin resolution, "to sending our American boys into combat in a war in which we have no business, which is not our war, into which we have been misguidedly drawn, which is being steadily escalated." That vote set the Congress inexorably on a path of erosion of Congressional power, which allowed the President to usurp the power. The Iraq Resolution further eroded Congressional power over war making.

Why? We unleashed the neocons, who propelled Bush to invade Afghanistan. Afghanistan had provided training camps for the Saudi invaders. But the Congress punished all the people of Afghanistan with endless devastation because Osama bin Laden had operated from this country. This war, at this writing, is still going on today because of that vote.

As I type this, Joe Biden says he is withdrawing the troops. The problems for democracy, as in Vietnam, after our withdrawal are the same in Afghanistan. Muslim extremism will soon dominate this country where we tried to bring regime change.

Worse, however, is what followed. Once President Bush and Vice President Cheney smelled blood, they decided to do regime change in Iraq. Bush and Company ignored the lessons of regime change efforts by Bill Clinton in Somalia. As George Santayana said, "Those who cannot remember the past are condemned to repeat it."

Bush came to Congress for a resolution to authorize use of military force in Iraq ONLY. The President believed he had the authorization because of our previous action on terror. On October 10–11, the House (296–133) and the Senate (77–23) supported invasion of Iraq. Seventeen years later we are mourning the deaths of thousands of Americans and untold millions of Afghanis, Iraqis, Syrians, Yemenis, and to what end?

No member of Congress should ever forget that he or she sent people to die for questionable purposes. I spent two years in the United States Navy during the Vietnam War, taking care of soldiers, sailors, and marines who came back from that war. I've sent men into battle by my statement of "fit for duty." I have in my desk drawer today the rubber stamps I used to decide men's fates. Memorial Day, for me, is a day to remember all those who "survived" the war with PTSD as well as obvious physical injuries.

The people have given Congress enormous responsibility by giving the duty to Congress to decide if our military should strike another country. Authoritarian leaders have led their countries into disaster in the past. The idea that killing endless civilians will make us safer is a dangerous delusion. We must not attack Venezuela or Iran or North Korea or Ukraine or China. Sending others to die for your safety is the ultimate "Yea" or "Nay." These votes sear deep scars into your memory that never really fade way. They can (and often do) influence how your representative votes from that day forward.

John and Amo:
Two Shining Examples

A S I WAS GOING out this morning to get my 10,000 steps in, the sun was at my back. My shadow was seven feet tall. I thought it was a beautiful image for the shadow each of us casts on the face of the earth each day. I liked it because it was bigger than me but as I walked my image shrank and by the time I finished my workout, my shadow was three feet tall. It raised the question of what kind of shadow do we cast and how long does it last.

Before I continue, I'll admit, in this book I have said several not very flattering things about the people drawn to Congress. But occasionally, a person of such high morals and unquestionable integrity takes the oath, and if you are lucky enough to be represented by such a person, cherish it. It doesn't happen very often.

Today, I was thinking of the shadows of two of my friends who passed away recently, John

Lewis (D-GA) and Amo Houghton (R-NY). They were great friends and close allies in forming the Faith and Politics Group in the House of Representatives. They collaborated in the beginning of the House participation in the annual trip to Alabama to recreate the Edmund Pettus Bridge crossing from the 1960s.

Amo was warm and down-to-earth despite being probably the richest man in the House. It never showed. I felt a personal connection to Amo, which I never told him about. My grandfather was a bottler-blower for the Thatcher Milk bottle company in Streator, Illinois. Thatcher bought the Owens company, which had a mechanical bottle blower that put my grandfather out of work. Owens Glass was ultimately bought by Corning Glass. This company, Corning, had been controlled by Amo and his family since 1851. Amo was the fifth generation to be president of the company.

But I always watched Amo as he voted on the Ways and Means Committee on workers issues. He often broke with the Gingrich company line and voted for workers.

One day he surprised me and voted Newt's way. I kidded him gently about his vote. I said, "I'll bet you never treated your employees at Corning that way." He hung his head and said, "Jim, they have told me if I don't vote the lead-

er's way, they will take me off this committee."
He was truly embarrassed by the vote. I can't
even remember the issue now, but I will never
forget the look of anguish on his face.

Sometime later I got a call from Amo. He
began with no introductory pleasantries, which
were his specialty. He said, "I need a favor, and
don't say no." He went on to tell me about being
the American leader of a trilateral group of leg-
islators including British and Germans.

At that time in the House, Newt Gingrich
was dead set against members of the House
being involved in foreign travel or exchanges. He
cut all the travel budgets, and he alone decided
who could go anywhere for any purpose. Isola-
tionism did not start with Trump. Newt decreed
that all Congressional delegations had to have
a Democrat included, so that there could be no
claim of Republican boondoggling.

Amo went on to tell me that both the British
and German delegations were afraid that the US
was drifting away from our bonds with our allies
in Europe. "Jim," he pleaded, "I have asked all
my Democratic friends, and I'm down to you.
You know you are not on Newt's "A-list." Please
say, 'yes.'"

No one could say "no"' to the sincerity of
Amo. He was a prince who wore his crown
lightly. On that trip I saw Buckingham palace

and Churchill's estate as well as visiting with colleagues to the Hermitage Museum in St. Petersburg.

At the end he gave each of us a snuggly purple jacket that commemorated the US-British-German Conference. I treasure it and wear it in the fall in Seattle. Most people in Seattle mistake it for University of Washington Husky purple, but it is the color of my royal relationship with Amo. He is as close to a prince as I will ever know. I'll never forget Amo.

For twelve years I sat next to John Lewis on the Ways and Means Committee. He was not interested in making a name for himself by the legislation he wrote. Rather, he was interested in doing what was best for people. We often talked about the effects that various pieces of legislation had on ordinary people. This was the guiding principle of his vote on all legislation.

He came to the hearings prepared with his remarks and questions, and since he followed me in the order of speaking, he would often say that he liked the direction I had taken in my five minutes of speech and questioning. He was selfless, in that he could give credit to others and did not seek to dominate the issue. He simply wanted to stand up for the right principle, no matter the impact on him.

He had big companies in his city, like Coca-Cola and CNN, but he was always interested in how the law would impact the workers who he represented. He would not pander to anyone. I had plenty of time at his elbow to watch him deal with people. He was polite to all of them, whether they were press, lobbyists, or constituents. He always took time to talk to and shake hands with kids. He drove his staff crazy because it always took so long for him to move.

What you saw as his image was what he really was. I can't remember a single time in my time on the Committee with him when he showed another side to himself. The chairman, Danny Rostenkowski, who was the consummate old-time pol from Chicago, wanted him on the Committee. Danny was never sure how John might vote, but he trusted him.

John came to Seattle to help my campaigns on several occasions. Most memorable was his trip to do a fundraiser for me. In advance, I had given him a book entitled, *Not on American Soil*, which was a book written about one of the most egregious miscarriages of justice to soldiers going to fight in war for their country. It happened at Fort Lawton in Seattle. There were Italian prisoners of war housed next to the barracks of a company of Black stevedores headed to Iwo Jima the next day. Drinking and a fight occurred. In the morning an Italian was found hanged in a tree nearby.

The US government wanted to sweep this under the rug as quickly as possible. Leon Jaworski, of later Watergate fame and the Nuremburg trials, was sent to do the investigation and trial. With little evidence or witnesses and one defense counsel for twenty men, all were convicted of some part in the "lynching" of an Italian prisoner of war. Our troops had recently begun fighting their way up the Italian boot. The top military people did not want a PR disaster. The trial was quick and deeply flawed in terms of due process. All the defendants received bad conduct discharges that followed them all their lives. Several were sent to Leavenworth.

John helped me get the Army to reverse, posthumously, the bad conduct discharges. When he came to Seattle, he wanted to see the place where all this occurred. I'll never forget walking through the area at Fort Lawton. No one was too small or forgotten for John to stop and remember their suffering.

On another occasion, he met with a nine-year old black boy who came to testify to the Congress about the need for health care for his caregiver, his grandmother. They were from my district.

Humanity and love for all, without respect for politics, emanated from him at all times. If he were here, he would deny it, but he is as close to a saint as I have ever known. He walked in Christ's footsteps with every step he took.

THINKING ABOUT THE
END AT THE BEGINNING

THE WIFE OF A colleague (Heather Foley) was going through some of her husband's papers and sent me a copy of a letter he wrote about me. She asked me if I was still interested in the subject of the letter.

Tom Foley was a great friend and mentor from 1970, when I met him in my first race for the Washington State Legislature, until he died in 2013. We had many opportunities to work together over the years. When I first came to Congress in 1989, the anti-Japanese sentiment was quite intense in Washington, D.C.

The Japanese economy was dominant then, and Japanese products were flooding the markets from automobiles to high-tech electronic equipment. A congresswoman from Maryland got so exercised by this fact that she organized a demonstration on the steps of the House, in which people with baseball bats smashed

Toshiba TVs. The anger was palpable and counterproductive.

I came from Seattle which had a large contingent of Japanese Americans who had been interned in the camps in 1941 and had then gone out and fought for the United States in Italy. The 442nd combat unit composed of these brave men was the most highly decorated unit in the history of World War II.

I went to Tom and asked what I could do to help control this aggression against the Japanese. He said, "I'll put you on some exchanges with the Japanese. This not for resume building. You must go to the meetings and participate." In the course of this activity, I went to Japan more than forty times over the twenty-eight years I served.

On one occasion I led a delegation to Hiroshima on December 7, 1991. Tom's idea, along with the President of Sony, was that we should show a counter narrative to the angry response on the fiftieth anniversary of Pearl Harbor.

Several years earlier, Tom tasked me with looking at the HIV-AIDS epidemic and its potential impacts on the US and the world. Once his wife asked me if she could accompany me on one of my twenty-nine trips to India. She told me that as a high school student in the 1950s she had driven across India with her family. Her father was a USAID official and she wanted to return to some of the places she and Tom went on their honeymoon after getting married in Sri Lanka. I agreed, and then she said, "Tom doesn't like travel to anyplace but Japan. He will go to Japan at a moment's notice."

Tom's interest and knowledge of Japan was so complete that, with no hesitation, Bill Clinton sent him to be the Ambassador to Japan. I watched my mentor develop his ties to Japan, and I tried to emulate his behavior. I traveled to more than ninety percent of the states of India. I met all the Prime Ministers and Finance Ministers and minister related to the Aviation industry. Boeing was headquartered in my district and sold both military and commercial planes to the GOI (government of India). So both my world health interests and economic interests made it a logical place for me to focus.

I also met all the American ambassadors and stayed in the residence frequently. I formed the India Caucus in the House and was chair several times. I loved India's diverse and complex culture, which is made up of six major religions in a population that is four times the US population living in a land mass one-third the size of the US.

I talked to Bill Clinton about the possibility of being appointed ambassador to India by Hillary if she were elected. She did not win the nomination. Barack Obama won, but Tom wrote a letter to him, recommending me for the position.

I was a supporter of Hillary, so my stock was not high with the White House staff. Eventually, Obama appointed a fine Indian American, Richard Verma. Tom's letter is appended. I don't remember ever seeing it, but I told my kids to save it and read it at my funeral. It sounded like my mentor was proud of me. I told Heather Foley that I still was in love with India and would love to go work on the COVID-19 epidemic, which is ravaging India today. I also expressed my doubts that an eighty-four-year old former congressman had much of a chance to be ambassador. She said, "I'll write a cover letter and send it to Joe Biden."

I told this story to one of my junior colleagues and suggested that if he found a country he really liked, he should become the expert on the country in the Congress. One does not know in life what fate will put at your door. Foley and Mansfield in Japan, or Sasser from Tennessee in China, or Foglietta from Philadelphia in Rome.

They say all members of Congress are like the mouth of the Mississippi river: a mile wide and a half-inch deep. Knowing places and subject matter in depth is essential if we are to lead the world in business, human rights, peace, and war. One must think from the beginning about how you would like to leave your mark at the end. If you don't aim high, you will hit nothing.

April 13, 2009

Dear Mr. President:

I am writing to express my support for your nominating Congressman Jim McDermott to be our next Ambassador to India. I have had the pleasure of knowing him for over twenty years and I think the special relationships he has developed while visiting India at a time when it has evolved from a planned economy to a more open and capitalist society makes him unusually well qualified to be nominated.

As a statesman and respected leader in the US House of Representatives, and as a medical doctor and psychiatrist with a significant international portfolio and perspective, Jim McDermott has always been a voice for reason, hope, compassion and Democracy throughout his 20+ years in Congress. I'm proud to say that I recognized his abilities early on during my tenure as Speaker of the House. For instance, I felt such confidence in his integrity that I appointed him head of the Ethics Committee. And, I asked him to lead an international Congressional effort to explore how to alert other countries to the growing threat of HIV/AIDS.

It was because of this effort that Congressman Jim McDermott found himself engaging in intense diplomacy to convince international leaders of the importance of this disease and was able to persuade many important foreign countries to devote more resources to the epidemic and to help reinforce the efforts of the very few he found working to alleviate the problem. It was this quest that earned him the respect of his colleagues and of leaders and governments around the world, especially in India.

Once he had discovered India and its importance as a young Democracy and realized the determination of its political leaders to open it up to trade and capitalism he helped found the Congressional Caucus on India and Indian Americans. This caucus which he nurtured and nudged along has grown to become the largest caucus in the House of Representatives. It has attracted Democrats and Republicans, liberals and conservatives, along with Members from rural and urban America. His active efforts in its establishment show that he is a leader with an ability to bridge any divide and unite diverse people and viewpoints around a common goal.

I should mention, as an aside to reinforce my view that Jim McDermott is extremely talented with a willingness to devote hours to detail that as chairman of the House Ways and Means Income Security and Family Support Subcommittee, he developed legislation which you signed into law as part of the economic stimulus bill to extend unemployment benefits and to modernize our aging unemployment insurance system to better meet the needs of the American people in the 21st Century. He has also been a passionate voice and champion on behalf of foster children and vulnerable families across America. Just last year, under his guidance the Congress passed and President Bush signed the most sweeping reform of the child welfare system in well over a decade.

Since 1990, Jim McDermott has made countless trips to India and has made a point of visiting almost every individual state in that large country. He accompanied President Clinton on his trip to India and Pakistan and convinced me to allow the sitting Prime Minister Pamulaparthi Venkata Narasimha Rao to address a Joint Session of Congress in 1994. Jim McDermott's interest in India would be very well accepted by the Indian Government and his knowledge of the very difficult issues that involve our relationship with India would be most helpful to you and the Secretary of State in determining how to resolve the tense relations between India and Pakistan. He knows the history of the entire region and is sensitive to the interests of both Muslims and Hindus.

I believe that America's Ambassador to India must faithfully represent our ideals and hope for peace, while promoting our strategic interests in the region. We know there are no quick or easy solutions to the problems and threats confronting us, especially with respect to the Indian Subcontinent. I have every confidence that Congressman Jim McDermott will set an example in India and the region at the precise moment in time when America needs to reassess its global leadership.

It is because of Jim McDermott's real and continuing interest in India, his knowledge and understanding of its politics and economy that I recommend him to you to become your nominee as the next Ambassador to India.

Best regards.
Sincerely,
Thomas S. Foley

Former Speaker of the U. S. House
of Representatives and former
U. S. Ambassador to Japan

ABOUT THE AUTHOR

Written by Brad Holden

Reprinted courtesy of HistoryLink.org.
For more information, visit *https://historylink.org/File/20961.*

JIM MCDERMOTT WAS A titan in Washington state and national politics for nearly 50 years. An Illinois-born doctor who served in the U.S. Navy as a psychiatrist during the Vietnam War, McDermott made his first foray into politics in 1970, when he was elected to the Washington State House of Representatives at age 33. After a failed run for governor two years later, he won a state senate seat in 1974, held it until 1987, and then was elected to the U.S. House of Representatives in 1988. A liberal Democrat representing Seattle's 7th Congressional District, McDermott championed universal healthcare, was an architect of the Affordable Care Act of 2010, and staunchly opposed the wars in

Iraq and Afghanistan. He suffered perhaps his biggest setback in 2008, when a federal judge ordered him to pay more than $1.1 million to fellow Congressman John Boehner after Boehner sued McDermott for releasing the contents of an illegally recorded cellphone call. When he retired in 2016 after 14 terms in Washington, D.C., McDermott was saluted by President Barack Obama as "a much-needed voice for the nation's most vulnerable."

ILLINOIS BORN AND RAISED

James Adelbert McDermott was born on December 28, 1936 in Chicago, Illinois. His father, William McDermott, worked as an underwriter for an insurance company, and his mother, Roseanna, when not busy raising a family, worked as a switchboard operator for a telephone company. McDermott was raised with three siblings in the Chicago suburb of Downers Grove. As a boy he had a strong intellectual curiosity about how things worked; once he discovered something interesting, he wanted to examine and understand it from all angles. This inquisitive drive would stay with him, as would the moral code from his early religious teachings. His parents were devout members of the Independent Fundamentalist Church of America (IFCA), and the family regularly attended service at the Southtown Bible Church. McDermott credits this strict religious upbringing with shaping his progressive worldview, as his interpretation of the scriptures centered around helping the poor and downtrodden (Brad Holden interview).

McDermott graduated Downers Grove High School in 1954, and was the first person in his family to attend college, at Wheaton College in Illinois, followed by the University of Illinois College of Medicine, where he earned an M.D. in 1963. During these academic years, he married Virginia Beattie (b. 1938) in 1961. McDermott, always fascinated with the human mind, earned a degree in psychiatry after completing a two-year residency at the University Of Illinois Research Hospital.

In 1966, he and his wife moved to Seattle after scouting out other cities. He was attracted to the cultural ambiance of Seattle, as well as its surrounding natural beauty. As he recalled, "It was a vibrant small city" (Holden interview). The McDermotts established their new home, arriving with their 1-month-old baby girl, Katherine. They would later welcome a son, James, in 1968. During this time, McDermott pursued fellowship training in child psychiatry at the University of Washington Medical Center, which he completed in 1968.

After his fellowship training, McDermott was drafted into the U.S. Navy. He served as a psychiatrist in the Navy Medical Corps from 1968 through 1970. This was during the Vietnam War, and McDermott was assigned to the Long Beach Naval Station in California, where he helped returning soldiers deal with combat-related trauma. This experience, seeing first-hand the mental and physical toll the war was taking, hardened McDermott's antiwar stance. This sentiment emboldened him: The day after being honorably discharged from the Navy, he promptly filed for political office, and thus began the next phase of his life.

EARLY POLITICAL CAREER

McDermott had long been inspired by such political figures as Thomas Jefferson, Franklin D. Roosevelt and Tommy Douglas (1904–1986) — the Canadian politician who introduced the continent's first single-payer, universal health care program — and was determined to help make a positive difference in people's lives (Holden interview). He made his first run for public office in 1970, and was elected to the Washington State Legislature as a Representative from the 43rd District, becoming the first

Democrat to win this particular seat. Post-election press releases celebrated his upset victory by exclaiming, "There's a fresh breeze blowing in Washington — Jim McDermott. And he has never heard of the word 'can't.'"

In March 1972, McDermott announced his candidacy for governor. He acknowledged his underdog status, but as he stated at a news conference, "To me and others, this is not an impossible dream" ("McDermott Enters ..."). He adopted the slogan "Not For Sale" and campaigned heavily against his opponents seeking the Democratic nomination, including former governor Albert D. Rosellini (1910–2011) and state senator Martin J. Durkan (1923–2005). In the end, Rosellini would clinch the primary to become the Democratic nominee against Republican incumbent governor Dan Evans (b. 1925), who would go on to win re-election.

In 1974, McDermott once again placed his hat in the political ring when he ran for state senator in the 43rd District. He handily won this election and would hold his seat for four successive terms, until 1987. During his time in the state senate, he crafted and sponsored legislation that would become known as the Washington State Basic Health Plan, the first such program in the nation to offer health insurance to the unemployed and the working poor. He was the author of the Basic Education Act, and worked toward reforming the nursing-home industry and making improvements in mental-health programs.

In 1980, while a state senator, McDermott ran again for governor, defeating incumbent Dixy Lee Ray (1914–1994) in the Democratic primary. He would later lose the general election to Republican John Spellman (1926–2018). In 1984, McDermott made a final run for governor when he ran on his so-called "APPLE Agenda" — an acronym for Affordable health care, Promotion of jobs, Protection of natural resources, Life with hope and without fear, and Excellence in education. He lost the primary to Booth Gardner (1936–2013), who then defeated Spellman in the general election.

After the loss, McDermott left politics and returned to medicine, becoming a Foreign Service medical officer based in Zaire (now the Democratic Republic of the Congo) and providing psychiatric services to Foreign Service and Peace Corps personnel in Africa from 1987 through 1988.

THE LIBERAL LION OF SEATTLE

Upon his return from Africa, McDermott, motivated by a desire to create a national healthcare system, decided to re-enter politics. He ran for Washington's 7th Congressional District in the U.S. House of Representatives when the seat came open in 1988 after incumbent Mike Lowry (1939–2017) gave it up to run for the U.S. Senate. McDermott won the election with 71 percent of the vote. He would go on to win re-election 13 times, firmly holding his seat until his retirement in 2016. During his tenure in Congress, McDermott served on the Budget Committee, the House Ethics Committee, and was a ranking senior member of the House Ways and Means Committee. He founded and chaired the Congressional Task Force on International HIV/AIDS, sat on the Medicare Commission, and was a member of the House Progressive Caucus.

In 1990, during his first term in Congress, McDermott authored the AIDS Housing Opportunity Act, which provides local governments with resources to meet the housing needs of those with AIDS. In subsequent years McDermott would be the primary author of several other bills enacted into law. These include the Medicare Beneficiary Enrollment Improvement Act; the Restoration of Emergency Unemployment Compensation Act of 2010; the Worker, Homeownership and Business Assistance Act of 2009; the Unemployment Compensation Extension Act of 2008; the SSI Extension for Elderly and Disabled Refugees Act; the Cedar River Watershed Land Exchange Act of 1992; and H.R. 5302, which designated the United States Courthouse located on 5th Avenue in Seattle as the "William Kenzo Nakamura United States Courthouse."

McDermott said he was particularly proud of the Cedar River Watershed Act, which allowed Seattle total control of its primary water source and was one of the last laws signed by President George H. W. Bush before he left office. Other bills that he authored into law include the African Growth and Opportunity Act, a trade policy that assisted African countries, and the Fostering Connections to Success and Increasing Adoptions Act — the first law to recognize the needs of foster children who were aging out of the system. Being a longtime advocate of a single-payer healthcare system, McDermott was one of the chief architects of the Affordable Care Act of 2010 (commonly known as Obamacare).

THE GINGRICH TAPE

In January 1997, McDermott found himself at the center of controversy when an illegally recorded phone call was leaked to several media outlets, including *The New York Times*. At the time, Speaker of the House Newt Gingrich was under investigation for giving inaccurate information to the House Ethics Committee regarding his use of tax-exempt funds. During the investigation, a married couple from Ft. White, Florida claimed they had picked up a cellphone conversation on their police scanner, which they then recorded on a hand-held recorder. The phone call included a discussion between Gingrich and his attorneys in which they could be heard strategizing about how to undercut the Ethics Committee's case against the speaker. Two other Republican politicians could also be heard on the phone call, including Representative John Boehner (b. 1949) and House majority leader Dick Armey. The Florida couple, John and Alice Martin, decided that the call might be important for the Ethics Committee and handed a recording of the call to McDermott, the senior Democrat on the committee. McDermott forwarded the tape to his fellow committee members, though the material on the tape was refused at the direction of Republican chairperson Nancy Johnson and was instead forwarded to the U.S. Justice Department. Charges were then brought against the couple for violating the Communications Privacy Act.

Two days later, on January 10, 1997, a transcript of the tape appeared on the front page of *The New York Times* and McDermott was later revealed to be the source. Republicans demanded an investigation into the leak and the matter was brought before the Justice Department. No legal charges were ever brought against McDermott, prompting Boehner to file a lawsuit in March 1998, in which he sought punitive damages from McDermott for disclosing an illegally intercepted call under the Electronic Communications Privacy Act.

The ensuing legal fight would last a decade as the case was dragged through various courts. In the end, U.S. District Judge Thomas Hogan ruled in favor of Boehner, and McDermott was ordered to pay legal restitution to Boehner. McDermott appealed, arguing that his actions were allowed under the First Amendment. A total of 18 news organizations, including CBS, ABC, NBC, CNN, The Associated Press, *The New York Times*, and the *Washington Post*, filed a joint legal brief backing McDermott. Despite the widespread support, the appeals court ruled in favor of Boehner. McDermott continued his efforts to appeal the decision, with the case eventually making its way to the Supreme Court, which declined to review the case. On March 1, 2008, with his legal avenues exhausted, McDermott was ordered to pay Boehner more than $1 million in legal costs, plus an additional $60,000 in damages.

In a statement to the media after the final decision, McDermott stated that the legal fight was worth it and that "while the amount of damages assessed in this case is significant, I submit that defending the First Amendment is beyond measure and worth every penny" ("Taped-Call Case ...").

WEAPONS OF MASS DESTRUCTION

In 2002, while Congress debated a war resolution act authorizing the use of force in Iraq, McDermott gained national attention when he proclaimed that President George W. Bush was misleading the country about Iraq's nuclear weapons arsenal, the presence of which was being used by the White House as pretext for launching an invasion. In addition to his comments, McDermott voted against the Iraq War, causing political opponents to nickname him "Baghdad Jim." The country eventually went to war. Years later, international intelligence reports would conclude that while a few random chemical weapons were found, no biological or nuclear weapons were discovered in Iraq, supporting McDermott's original claims.

McDermott maintained his opposition to the wars in Iraq and Afghanistan, and curated an ongoing photo display outside his office showing Washington state soldiers who died in Iraq and Afghanistan. He titled the display, "Washington Faces of the Fallen," saying its purpose was to make sure they were not forgotten. Every time a soldier from Washington died in combat, he would add their photo. By the time he left office in 2016, there were more than 150 of them.

PLEDGE OF ALLEGIANCE

On April 28, 2004, McDermott again found himself at the center of controversy when he omitted the phrase "under God" while leading the House of Representatives in reciting the Pledge of Allegiance. Two years earlier, a decision by the 9th U.S. Circuit Court of Appeals ruled that it was unconstitutional to have school children recite the Pledge of Allegiance in class because it included the words "under God." In response, the Republican-led House of Representatives had overwhelmingly approved two resolutions expressing outrage over Circuit Court ruling. McDermott's omission of the two words was seen as an escalation of the issue.

The words "under God" had first been added to the Pledge of Allegiance in 1954, during the height of the McCarthy era when Congress passed a bill that was signed into law. McDermott, who was a high school senior in 1954, maintained that his version of the Pledge was what he learned in school and was the one he accepted personally.

'A Much-Needed Voice'

On January 4, 2016, McDermott announced his retirement, stating that he would not be seeking another term. When interviewed by the local media he explained, "I've seen people leave Congress in handcuffs. I've seen them die. I've seen them defeated. And then there's a few who walk out. And I thought to myself, 'That option seems like a better option'" ("Political Pack Rat Boxes Up ...").

Upon hearing of McDermott's decision to retire, President Barack Obama praised McDermott saying that he'd been "a much-needed voice for the nation's most vulnerable." House minority leader and former speaker Nancy Pelosi applauded McDermott's accomplishments, stating, "Whether in the U.S. Navy Medical Corps during the Vietnam War, as a foreign service medical officer, or as a champion of single-payer healthcare, Jim made it his life's work to ensure quality healthcare is available to every American, not just the privileged few." In his farewell speech, McDermott told his colleagues they'll face "a dark and difficult road," but he urged them to confront a "menacing wave of nativism, misogyny and racism that is raging in our country."

Drawing on his 46-year political career, McDermott spent part of his post-retirement life teaching a foreign policy course at the University of Washington's Jackson School of International Studies. The school was always in McDermott's district, and teaching there seemed fitting. He and Virginia divorced in 1989, and a second marriage, to Therese Hansen, ended in 2011. McDermott enjoys working on Japanese ink wash paintings in his spare time, in a style known as Sumi-e. He also enjoys traveling; he purchased a rural house in the Bordeaux region of France, where he spends part of his time writing a book that he explains will serve as a manual for aspiring politicians to "better understand the system" (Holden interview).

McDermott navigated "the system" for 46 years with an autodidactic approach to understanding the world, combined with political idealogies picked up from the New Deal Democrats he admired. While he suffered his share of defeats, he also helped to define Seattle's political identity for decades. Part of his worldview is explained with a quote from the character Gandalf in J. R. R. Tolkien's "Lord of the Rings" trilogy. It is a quote McDermott used in his retirement speech, and which he still references today:

"It is not our part to master all the tides of the world, but to do what is in us for the succor of those years wherein we are set, uprooting the evil in the fields that we know, so that those who live after may have clean earth to till. What weather they shall have is not ours to rule" (Tolkien, *The Return of the King*).

This essay made possible by:

Microsoft Corporation

Seattle Office of Arts & Culture

King County

Sources: "Candidates File for State, County Posts," The Seattle Times, August 1, 1970, pg. 9; "Municipal League Considers Candidates," Ibid., August 30, 1970, pg. 86; Richard W. Larsen, "Labor Endorses Republican, 19 Democrats," Ibid., October 6, 1970, pg. 5; Richard W. Larson, "McDermott Enters Governor Race," Ibid., March 21, 1972, pg. 25; Richard W. Larson, "Peculiar New Political Winds Leave Evans Camp Uneasy," Ibid., September 24, 1972, pg. 10; "Candidates Start Filing," Ibid., July 30, 1974, pg. 30; Richard W. Larson, "Spellman, In Late Surge, Wins Governorship," Ibid., November 5, 1980, pg. 25; Richard W. Larson, "All That Conventional Political 'Wisdom,'" Ibid., December 28, 1980, pg. A19; "What Makes Politics Downright Delicious," Ibid., May 31, 1984, pg. 13; Dean Katz, "Gardner Maintains Lead in Fund-Raising, Ibid., August 28, 1984, pg. 1; "Q&A: Spellman, Gardner, McDermott," Ibid., September 9, 1984, pg. 20; Doug Underwood, "Steamrolled Liberals Seeks Solace in Reagan Era," Ibid., January 20, 1985, pg. B1; Eric Pryne, "Out Of Africa, McDermott Hits the Ground Running," Ibid., March 30, 1988, pg. C1; Susan Gilmore, "McDermott is Raising Money Fastest —Finances Disclosed for 7th District Race," Ibid., July 19, 1988, pg. B1; David Schaefer, "McDermott Plans Health Care Bill," Ibid., August 13, 1988, pg. A11; Susan Gilmore, "McDermott's Taking No Chances in 7th," Ibid., November 2nd, 1988, pg. H1; David Schaefer, "McDermott Seeking U.S. Aid to Fight AIDS in Africa," Ibid., August 28, 1990, pg. E2; Dick Lilly, "Watershed's End Run Worked," Ibid., August 25,

1993, pg. B2; Danny Westneat, "Civil Suit Against McDermott Over Leaked Tape Gears Up — Rep. Boehner Says His Privacy Was Violated," Ibid., May 19, 1998, pg. A10; James V. Grimaldi, "McDermott May Have to Break Silence — Judge's Ruling Could End Mystery of Leaked Tape," Ibid., July 18, 1998, pg. A1; Erik Lacitis, "Let Hawks Screech; Many Back McDermott," Ibid., October 3, 2002, pg. C1; David Postman, "McDermott Accuses Bush of Plotting to Become Emperor — Back Home, He Renews His Attack on War Plans," Ibid., October 7, 2002, pg. B1; Jim Brunner and Alex Fryer, "McDermott Leads Pledge in House, Omits 'Under God' — Gap in Recitation Raises Republican Heckles," Ibid., April 29, 2004, pg. A1; Matthew Daly, "Taped-Call Case Ends With Payment," Ibid., April 29, 2008, pg. B2; Emily Heffter, "McDermott Again Appears Untouchable," Ibid., August 14, 2008, pg. B10; Lance Dickie, "The GOP is on the Wrong Side of the Nation's Health-Care Debate," Ibid., November 13, 2009, p. A14; Danny Westneat, "Liberal Lion Worked Across The Aisle," Ibid., January 6, 2016, pg. B3; Nicole Brodeur, "Political Pack Rat Boxes Up The Memories," Ibid., December 6, 2016, pg. B1; Lisette Alvarez, "Congressman Sues a Colleague Over Disclosing G.O.P. Talks," The New York Times, January 15, 1997, pg. 2; Jerry Gray, 'Florida Couple Are Charged in Taping of Gingrich Call," Ibid., April 24, 1997, pg. 5; Edwin Chen, "McDermott Will Quit Panel Over Speaker Flap," Los Angeles Times, January 15, 1997, pg. 5; Charles Pope, "McDermott Defends His Patriotism," Seattle Post-Intelligencer, October 2, 2002, pg. 4; Mike Romano, "The Unbearable Lightness of Jim McDermott," Seattle Weekly, October 9, 2006; Various facts from (https://www.house.gov/), (https://ballotpedia.org/Jim_McDermott_(Washington), (https://www.congress.gov/member/jim-mcdermott), (https://www.ontheissues.org/House/Jim_McDermott.htm); Brad Holden Interviews with Jim McDermott; various one-on-one talks at McDermott's residence between December 14, 2019 and January 18, 2020.

PICTURES

Summer, 1961. I was a participant in OPERATION-Cross-roads AFRICA. I spent time in the town of Nkwatia, Ghana, building a two-room mud brick addition to St. Peters Academy and living as close to the ground as is possible for a kid from Chicago to get. I had a red beard and was known as Hajjad on the street. Traditionally anyone who has made the pilgrimage to Mecca is allowed to dye his beard red. This whole trip was my introduction to problems of the developing world. Malaria mosquitos, latrines, boiled drinking water, and the diet of village people. It was mostly starch and very heavily soaked in hot peppers. I lost 30 pounds, but I developed a love for the underprivileged of the world. My thanks to James Robinson, pastor of the Church of the Master in New York, who had a vision of the emergence of Africa from colonial rule. He talked to JFK about creating the Peace Corps.

Captain Joe Zuska, USN, and me, Long Beach Naval Station 1968. Joe was a Czech from my alma mater who never made admiral because he forced the US Navy to admit there was alcoholism among military officers. He made me chief of the first Alcoholic Rehab Clinic in the Navy. He was a great commanding officer.

Senator Henry Jackson helping my first campaign in 1970.
I was against the Vietnam war and Henry was a supporter,
but he went to the QFC grocery store in my district and told
people he was supporting me as they came out of the check out
line. (Senator Jackson served in the Senate from 1953–1983.)

Blaine, Washington, at the start of the of Governors race in 1972. I began the race with a 700 mile bicycle ride from Blaine to Vancouver, Washington. Nobody told me Lawton Childs walked the length of Florida and had a well-financed promotional campaign. My daughter, Kate, age 6, and son, Jim, age 3, had no idea what dad was doing. Don't forget your family.

Senator Warren Magnuson and me — M&M campaign, 1980, defeat for both by Reagan. Maggie loved the Senate and never once hankered after the Supreme Court or the Presidency. "I belong to the best club in the world and I'm staying." (Senator from Washington state 1944–1981.)

Best Wishes to the McDermott Family,

Jimmy Carter

November 4, 1980. Me, my son Jim, my wife Virginia, and the President, all smile on the night Jimmy Carter and I lost our races. Jimmy Carter then got on the plane and heard the final news. Learning to smile with tears in your eyes is an art.

To Jim McDermott
With best wishes,

Thomas J. Foley
(Speaker)

Tom Foley, friend, mentor, and "Last Speaker of the whole House." He presided over the House proceedings, not trying to control every outcome. He rode with a light hand on the reins of power. Speaker of the House from 1989–1995.

Christmas 1993, Bill and Hillary in White House. First White House Christmas party for President Clinton and me. Mrs. Clinton and I became good friends too because we worked for a whole year trying to get a vote on her Universal Health care package. The woman on the left is Muriel Dobbin, a reporter for the Baltimore Sun, and my date for the evening.

George H.W. Bush signing Puyallup Reservation/Port of Tacoma, H.R. 932. This is the classic photo of a freshman who wasn't aware you had to promote yourself. It was my bill in my subcommittee on the Interior Committee, designed to resolve all the land claims between the Port of Tacoma and the Puyallups. Without it the Port could expand anywhere. I didn't get myself in the picture, but Norm Dicks took care of me.

Dalai Lama in D.C. I saw him so many times and in many places that he rememberedf my face and would always playful-ly greet me.

Facetime talk with my friend, Dalai Lama, in Washington, D.C. The Dalai Lama was a friend who came often at the invitation of the Speaker, Nancy Pelosi.

Taveling with Bill and Chelsea Clinton in India, August 27, 2000. I travelled with President Clinton to Africa, South America, and to India. This trip was near the end of his eight years as President, and Mrs. Clinton had paved the way for him with a previous trip. He was received very warmly.

Speaking at the Nisei veterans recognition ceremony at the University of Washington, November 11, 2005, at Meany Hall. I was an Honorary Nisei vet, and we honored the Most Decorated Military Units of WWII, the 442nd Regimental Combat team. If you were too old to be in the battle you were assigned to be Military Intelligence. They were awarded more than 18,000 awards. Many never received their awards for whatever reason. They all came out of isolated concentration camps in the West to volunteer to serve. The Army was present at the ceremony, including General Richard Myers, the Chairman of the Joint Chiefs Of Staff, who spoke with Senator Daniel Inouye, who was a member. This was a memorable day for any vet.

SEATTLE UNIVERSITY FOSTERING SCHOLARS
OCTOBER 17TH, 2010

I was on the Ways and Means Committee, and I got dragged away from the Health Subcommittee by Charlie Rangel, who said I was trained in dealing with those less fortunate in life (in other words, poor kids, foster kids, and the disabled, mentally and emotionally, and those out of work). I rewrote the unemployment law for the first time since 1935, and also reworked a section of Title IV that dealt with dependent children who had been removed from their homes. I was the godfather for 500,000 foster kids in the US, and I saw all their problems. When we lowered the voting age to 18, most states lowered the age for taking care of kids to 18. Aging out of foster care with no support was a rude shock to many children. I changed the law so Federal money could continue to smooth the transition. People like Father Sundborg, S.J., at Seattle University, set up programs to help these kids make it. The proceeds of this book are directed to that program. I don't know their names, but they are a great bunch of tough resilient kids.

Raghad Bird and her family, she was a translator I helped rescue from the Shia Militia in Baghdad. Casework in Congress is one of the most rewarding activities you do. Raghad Bird came to me to get help for her mother who was trapped in Iraq. Raghad and her brother had worked with the US Military translating for them. She and her brother were targeted for assassination by the Shia militia. We got her and all her family out to Jordan but the US was unwilling to take her mother's word that the children were hers without birth certificates, so they could not come to the US. This fierce mother went back into Iraq and went to Baghdad to get the documents. When she arrived back at the Jordanian border, Jordan immigration would not let her out of Iraq. Here is where Rita Patel, from my staff, stepped in and made it happen. Nobody gets anything done without staff help.

At her retirement party, Jane Sanders, a great chief of staff, said, "NO gifts. I just want a photo of everyone who worked with me." Everyone made it at 8:00 A.M. except one woman who had a dental appointment. For years these people took care of 700,000 people, including me. They got me out of trouble or anticipated problems. All my success goes to them, and a similar group in Washington, D.C. Any member who forgets this truth is headed for problems. My heartfelt thanks to you all.

Charles "Mike" Williams, 1988 campaign manager and Chief of Staff (COS) for 10 years. He wrote the African Growth and Opportunity Act (AGOA) Trade policy for Africa. He worked for SNCC in the 1960s, and got a PHD without thesis from UMASS Amherst. He was the smartest COS that ever worked in Washington, D.C. He was street smart and saved me from stuff but also came up with brilliant ideas to get stuff done. I could write a whole chapter about staff ideas I stole that made me look good.

Left Coast Dinner Group met at the Hunan Dynasty almost every week. Tom Downey, George Miller, Barbara Boxer, Nancy Pelosi, Sam Farr, Sam Gjedensen, Chuck Schumer, John Lewis, Pete Stark, Anna Eschoo, and me (absent Bernie Sanders and Dick Durbin). We came from all over country, and were on all the committees so we always knew what had or was going to happen. The only hassles were around who paid for dinner. Some were more generous than others. This was similar to descriptions of dinners in the old days. Eating together is a bonding experience and helps to keep people out of trouble.

Obama Inauguration, January 20, 2013, on West Front of the Capitol. Standing next to me with the hat is Bobby Rush, former Black Panther leader from Chicago, who beat Barack in his first run for Congress. It was not always a smooth road for President Obama, and Bobby said good things to me about him during the ceremony. But he did relish telling me about the race in 2000. We are all so competitive.

*We can solve all the problems — just need a
bottle and a paper sack —*

*I had many friends in Congress, but none better than Sam Farr,
who was a former Peace Corps volunteer from Columbia. We
were brothers from the day we met. On December 31, 2016,
he and I ended our careers in Congress at Point 16 on the Big
Sur, on the California coast, at his family summer place. As we
stood at midnight looking at the expanse of the Pacific Ocean
and the stars overhead, Sam turned to me and said, "Jim, you
and I are in the latest volume of Who's Who for 2016. When
we wake up, we will be, 'Who was he?'"*

9 780578 292724